*Chopin with Cherries*
*A Tribute in Verse*

# Chopin with Cherries
# A Tribute in Verse

*edited by*
Maja Trochimczyk

Los Angeles • Moonrise Press • 2010

This book is published by

**Moonrise Press**
P.O. Box 4288, Los Angeles – Sunland
CA 91041-4288, www.moonrisepress.com

© Copyright 2010 by Maja Trochimczyk
Introduction and three poems: "How to Make a Mazurka," "Harvesting Chopin" and "A Study with Cherries."

© Copyright 2010 by Maja Trochimczyk
Selection of content, layout, and design, including the cover design, using a fragment of Chopin postcard from Austria with a Lithuanian folksong, ca. 1900. Illustrations from Maja Trochimczyk Collection. Used by Permission. Photograph of a moon by Susan Rogers. Used by Permission.

© Copyright 2010 by Moonrise Press
All poetry content for this compilation only © by Moonrise Press. After the publication, copyright of individual poems reverts to each author. Prior publication of certain poems and permission to reprint these poems as listed is hereby gratefully acknowledged.

All Rights for this Compilation Only Reserved 2010 by Moonrise Press

*No part of this book may be reproduced or utilized in any form or by any means, electronic or mechanical, including photocopying and recording, or by any information storage and retrieval system, without permission in writing from the publisher.*

**Manufactured in the United States of America**

**The Library of Congress Publication Data:**

Trochimczyk, Maja, 1957–
    [Poems. English. Collections and Anthologies]
    Chopin with Cherries: A Tribute in Verse / Maja Trochimczyk, editor
        256 pages (xxxii pp. + 224 pp.) 15.2 cm x 22.9 cm.
        Written in English. Includes 123 poems by 92 poets, one translation from the Polish (Norwid's "Fortepian Szopena"), 50 illustrations, 7 portraits, the editor's introduction, and an index of poets.

    **ISBN 978-0-9819693-0-5** (paperback)

    I. Trochimczyk, Maja, 1957–Poetry. II. Title.

10 9 8 7 6 5 4 3 2 1

# TABLE OF CONTENTS

Prior Publications Credits (x)
Musical References (xi)

Maja Trochimczyk – *Introduction: The Poetry of Chopin in Poetry* (xiii)

## NAME (3)
1. Emma Lazarus – *Chopin* (4)
2. Amy Lowell – *Chopin* (6)
3. William Pillin – *Chopin* (8)
4. Millicent Borges Accardi – *Chopin* (11)
5. Alison Ross – *Chopin* (13)
6. Maxine R. Syjuco – *Chewing Chopin* (14)

## PIANO (15)
7. Cyprian Kamil Norwid – *The Piano of Chopin*
    *Fortepian Szopena* translated by Leonard Kress (16)
8. Charles Adés Fishman – *Chopin's Piano* (22)
9. Kerri Buckley – *Ruby and Sapphire* (23)
10. Martin Willitts Jr. – *The Enemy is in the House* (24)
11. Millicent Borges Accardi – *More Polish than Poland* (26)
12. Roxanne Hoffman – *G* (27)
13. Jessica Day – *I Tell My Piano the Things I Used to Tell You* (28)

## PRELUDES (29)
14. Leonard Kress – *A Minor Prelude* (30)
15. Christine Klocek-Lim – *Prelude in Majorca* (32)
16. Richard Pflum – *Raindrop Prelude* (34)
17. Cheryl M. Thatt – *Chopin's "Raindrop"* (35)
18. Ben Humphrey – *A Pastoral Piece in D-Flat Major* (36)
19. Carrie A. Purcell – *Prelude in D-flat Major, Op. 28, No. 15* (38)
20. Marianne Worthington – *Minor Detour through an
    Old Neighborhood* (39)
21. Nils Peterson – *After Listening to All the Preludes* (40)

## ETUDES (41)
22. Elisabeth Murawski – *Etude* (42)
23. Joseph Somoza – *Chopin Etude* (43)

24. R. Romea Luminarias – *There Is No Other Love* (44)
25. Maja Trochimczyk – *A Study with Cherries* (45)
26. Mark Tardi – *From First Part——Chopin's Feet* (47)

## MAZURKAS (53)
27. Kathi Stafford – *Mazurka, Formed of Rain* (54)
28. Katrin Talbot – *Sewing with Chopin* (56)
29. Maja Trochimczyk – *Harvesting Chopin* (57)
30. Katrin Talbot – *Mazurka vs. the Day* (58)
31. Maja Trochimczyk – *How to Make a Mazurka* (59)

## POLONAISES (61)
32. Elisabeth Murawski – *Polonaise* (62)
33. John Z. Guzlowski – *A Good Death* (64)
34. Gabriel Shanks – *Polonaise for Justyna* (66)
35. Kath Abela Wilson – *How I Fell in Love with Chopin* (67)

## WALTZES (69)
36. Lori Desrosiers – *Waltz* (70)
37. Lois P. Jones – *This Waltz is not for Dancing (Chopin's Waltz in A Minor, Posthumous)* (71)
38. Russell Salamon – *Waltz in A Minor* (72)
39. Dean Pasch – *Gdańsk (after Waltz in A Minor, Posthumous)* (73)
40. Ben Humphrey – *An Invitation in D-flat Major* (74)
41. Marlene Hitt – *Minute Waltz* (75)
42. Taoli-Ambika Talwar – *My One Minute Waltz* (77)
43. Clark Crouch, Cowboy Poet – *Chopin's Minute Waltz* (80)
44. Sharon Chmielarz – *Chopin: Thoughts a-Waltz* (81)
45. Taoli-Ambika Talwar – *Waltzing with Chopin in a Foreign Land* (82)
46. Emily Fragos – *19 Chopin Waltzes* (84)

## NOCTURNES (85)
47. Elisabeth Murawski – *Nocturne: Chopin in Vienna* (86)
48. Linda Nemec Foster – *Mazovian Willows* (88)
49. David Ellis – *Chopin's Sonnet (Nocturne in D-flat Major, Op. 27, No. 2)* (90)
50. Jarek Gajewski – *The Last Nocturne* (91)
51. Jennifer S. Flescher – *Waiting for Fingers for Keys* (92)

52. Rosemary O'Hara – *Nocturne No. 6 in G Minor*
    (after Nocturne in G Minor, Op. 15, No. 3) (93)
53. Lucy Anderton – *Night Nocturne* (95)
54. Kerri Buckley – *The Scarlet Hour* (97)
55. Lia Brooks – *During Nocturne (Nocturne in E Minor,*
    *Op. 72, No. 1)* (98)
56. Leonore Wilson – *Nocturnes in Spring* (100)
57. Marie Lecrivain – *Chopin's Nocturnes Askew* (101)
    *I. (after Nocturne in E-flat Major, Op. 9, No. 2)* (101)
    *II. (after Nocturne in E Major, Op. 62, No. 2)* (102)
    *III. (after Nocturne in C-sharp Minor, Op. 27, No. 1)* (103)
58. Lola Haskins – *Nocturne (after Chopin)* (104)
59. Victor Contoski – *Chopin Nocturne* (105)
60. Russell Salamon – *Eternal Nocturne* (106)

## SONATAS & OTHER WORKS (107)
61. Jean L. Kreiling – *Tryst (Chopin's Sonata for Cello*
    *and Piano Op. 65)* (108)
62. Shayla Hawkins – *Thunder of Sorrow (after Chopin's Piano Sonata*
    *in B-flat Minor, Opus 35, The Funeral March)* (109)
63. Meg Withers – *Berceuse, Opus 57 in D-Flat* (111)
64. Gretchen Fletcher – *Listening to Chopin's Ballades* (112)
65. Richard Pflum – *A Cry in the Woods (Fantasy Impromptu*
    *in C-sharp Minor)* (115)
66. Ruth Nolan – *Concerto No. 1, in E minor, on Highway 111,*
    *in Palm Springs* (116)

## LIFE (117)
67. Leonore Wilson – *Night-Blooming Jasmine* (118)
68. Jeffrey Levine – *Comprimario* (119)
69. Tammy L. Tillotson – *A Letter from Countess Wodzińska*
    *to her Daughter Maria, Winter, 1835* (120)
70. Tammy L. Tillotson – *A Letter from Maria Wodzińska*
    *to F. Chopin, September, 1836* (121)
71. Tammy L. Tillotson – *A Letter from Fryderyk Chopin*
    *to Himself, September, 1836* (122)
72. Kathi Stafford – *Second Movement* (123)
73. Beata Poźniak Daniels – *Twenty Six* (124)
74. Austin Alexis – *Chopin and Sand* (126)
75. Helen Graziano – *Chopinesque* (127)

76. Lusia Slomkowska – *Chopin in Mallorca* (129)
77. Erika Wilk – *Winter in Majorca* (130)
78. Martin Willitts, Jr. – *Discord* (131)
    I. *Chopin to George Sand, 1847* (131)
    II. *George Sand to "beloved little corpse"* (132)
79. Georgia Jones-Davis – *Chopin's Sorrow* (133)
80. Laura L. Mays Hoopes – *Goodbye to Poland* (135)
81. Carol J. Jennings – *Love Letter to Chopin* (136)

## DEATH (137)
82. George Bodmer – *In Which Thackeray's Daughter Visits the Dying Chopin* (138)
83. Jennifer S. Flescher – *Last Words (after reading Franz Liszt on Chopin's Death)* (139)
84. Kenneth Pobo – *October 17, 1849* (140)
85. Fiona Sze-Lorrain – *Chopin's Death Mask* (142)
86. Anne Harding Woodworth – *At the "Hour of Twilight"* (143)
87. Erika Wilk – *Everlasting Love* (145)
88. Radomir Vojtech Luza – *Frozen Flowers* (146)

## PLAYING (147)
89. Marilyn N. Robertson – *We speak Chopin* (148)
90. Mira N. Mataric – *Chopin and I* (149)
91. Donna L. Emerson – *Chopin and Church* (152)
92. Charlotte Jones – *Posthumous* (154)
93. Lois P. Jones – *Impressions: Mario's Chopin* (156)
94. Susan Rogers – *Alicia Plays Chopin* (157)
95. Martin Willitts, Jr. – *In the Music Stanzas* (159)
96. Sheila Black – *Exiles (3)* (161)
97. Donna L. Emerson – *Chopin in Ohio* (162)

## LISTENING (163)
98. T. S. Eliot – *Portrait of a Lady* (164)
99. Margaret Szumowski – *Concert at Chopin's House* (168)
100. Diane Shipley DeCillis – *Postcards of Home and Homesick* (169)
101. Sharon Chmielarz – *An American Hears Chopin* (171)
102. Thom Tammaro – *Chopin in North Dakota* (172)
103. Ryan McLellan – *Artsy Evening* (174)
104. Anna Maria Mickiewicz – *Chopin in Manchester* (175)
105. Rick Lupert – *Chopin in an Old Church* (176)

106. Peggy Castro – *Flight to Seattle* (177)
107. Ryan McLellan – *Chopin on the Radio* (178)
108. Helen Vandepeer – *Chopin in the Snow* (179)
109. Charlie Durrant – *He Sings Chopin, I Hum Brahms* (180)
110. Allison Campbell – *Chopin, Sheep, Feet* (182)
111. Marlene Hitt – *Fifteen Ways of Hearing a Wind Chime* (184)

## BEAUTY (187)

112. Mary Rudge – *When Isadora Duncan Danced Chopin* (188)
113. Davi Walders – *The Last Dance* (189)
114. Mira N. Mataric – *Dance with Me* (190)
115. Sharon Chmielarz – *Chopin: Apples* (191)
116. Katrin Talbot – *It's Been a Tough Symphony Week* (192)
117. Marian Kaplun Shapiro – *Eat when Hungry, Sleep when Tired* (193)
118. Leonore Wilson – *The Composer (after Chopin)* (195)
119. Radomir Vojtech Luza – *Beyond Utopia* (197)
120. Oriana Ivy – *Souvenirs* (198)
121. Kerri Buckley – *The Sounds of Chopin: A Villanelle* (200)
122. Elizabyth A. Hiscox – *Fryderyk Speaks to George of the Sky* (201)
123. Emily Fragos – *Chopiniana* (202)

Contributors (204)

Index of Poets (222)

## Prior Publication Credits

Prior publication of certain poems in the following books and journals is hereby gratefully acknowledged:

- Sheila Black's "Exiles (3)" was published in her book *Love/Iraq* (Cincinnati: CW Books, 2009).
- Diane Shipley DeCillis' *Postcards of Home and Homesick* was published in *The MacGuffin* (2008).
- T. S. Eliot's "Portrait of a Lady" was first published in *Others* magazine in 1915.
- Charles Adés Fishman's "Chopin's Piano" is the title poem of his book, *Chopin's Piano* (Time Being Books, 2006).
- Jennifer S. Flescher's "Last Words" appeared in *Scarab* and was nominated for a Pushcart Prize.
- Linda Nemec Foster's "Mazovian Willows" was published in her book, *Amber Necklace from Gdańsk* (Louisiana State University Press, 2001).
- Emily Fragos's "19 Chopin Waltzes" appeared in *The Cimarron Review* in 2006 and her "Chopiniana" in *Columbia: A Journal of Literature and Art.* (No. 43).
- Lola Haskins's "Nocturne: After Chopin" was published in her book, *The Rim Benders: Poems and Discourses* (Anhinga Press, 2001).
- Marian Kaplun Shapiro's "Eat When Hungrey, Sleep When Tired" was published in *Sacred Fire* (2006).
- Jeffrey Levine's "Comprimario" was included in *Rumor of Cortez* (Red Hen Press, 2005).
- Amy Lowell's Chopin was published in *Pictures of a Floating World* (McMillan Co., 1919).
- Rick Lupert's "Chopin in an Old Church" appeared in the book *I'd Like To Bake Your Goods* (Ain't Got No Press, January, 2006).
- Elisabeth Murawski's "Etude" first appeared in the online journal *Kritya :: In the Name of Poetry*.
- Rosemary O'Hara's "Nocturne No. 6 in G Minor" was in *Between the Lines* (2008).
- William Pillin's "Chopin" is reprinted from *To the End of Time: Poems New & Selected (1939-1979)* [Papa Bach Editions, 1980] by permission of Boris Pillin and Charles Adés Fishman.
- Richard Pflum's "A Cry in the Woods," was included in his chapbook, *Listening With Others* (2007).
- Alison Ross's "Chopin" was published in *A Little Poetry*.
- Joseph Somoza's "Chopin Etude" appeared in his book, *Out of This World* (El Paso: Cinco Puntos Press, 1990).

- Maxine R. Syjuco's "Chopin" was published in her book, *A Secret Life* (Art Quest World Wide, 2008).
- Fiona Sze-Lorrain's "Chopin's Death Mask" appears in *Water the Moon* (Marick Press, 2010).
- Margaret Szumowski's "Concert at Chopin's House" from *I Want This World* (Tupelo Press, 2001), used by permission of the publisher.
- Thom Tammaro's "Chopin in North Dakota" first appeared in *The Midwest Quarterly* (June 2004).
- Mark Tardi's 'Part First-----Chopin's Feet" is a fragment from his chapbook, *Part First-----Chopin's Feet,* published by g-o-n-g (2005).
- Maja Trochimczyk's "Harvesting Chopin" and "How to Make a Mazurka" were published in *Quill & Parchment* (No. 100, October 2009).
- Helen Vandepeer's "Chopin in the Snow" is a revised version of "Chopin" published in *The Goose River Press Anthology* (2009).
- Meg Withers' "Berceuse, Opus 57 in D-flat" was published in her book, *Must Be Present to Win* (Ghost Road Press, 2006).
- Marianne Worthington's "Minor Detour Through an Old Neighborhood" appeared in *Clapboard House: Artful Short Stories and Poems* (August 2008).

## Illustrations

All illustrations reproducing 19th and early 20th century Chopin postcards and Sigismond Ivanowski's engravings after Chopin Preludes are from privately owned Maja Trochimczyk Collection. Used by permission. Color images are available in downloadable pdf files of the book. The photograph of the moon by Susan Rogers in her poem, "Alicia Plays Chopin," is used by permission.

## Musical References

The following pieces by Fryderyk Chopin are cited or referred to in this volume:

- Berceuse in D-flat Major, Op. 57 – Meg Withers
- Concerto No. 1, in E Minor, Op. 11 – Ruth Nolan
- Concerto No. 2, in F Minor, Op. 21 – Donna L. Emerson
- Etude in C Major, Opus 10, No. 1 – Maja Trochimczyk
- Etude in E Major, Opus 10, No. 3 – Sheila Black, R. Romea Luminarias
- Fantasie Impromptu in C-sharp Minor, Op. 66 – Richard Pflum
- Mazurka in A Minor, Op. 17, No. 4 – Maja Trochimczyk
- Mazurka in F-sharp Minor, Op. 59, No. 3 – Maja Trochimczyk

- Nocturne in E-flat Major, Op. 9, No. 2 – Carol J. Jennings, Marie Lecrivain, Linda Nemec Foster
- Nocturen in F-sharp Major, Op. 15, No. 2 – postcard by Rzepkowski
- Nocturne in G Minor, Op. 15, No. 3 – Rosemary O'Hara
- Nocturne in C-sharp Minor, Op. 27, No. 1 – Marie Lecrivain
- Nocturne in D-flat Major, Op 27, No. 2 – David Ellis
- Nocturne in E Major, Op. 62, No. 2 – Marie Lecrivain
- Nocturne in E Minor, Op. 72, No. 1 – Lia Brooks
- Piano Sonata in B-flat Minor, Op. 35, The Funeral March – Donna L. Emerson and Shayla Hawkins
- Sonata for Cello and Piano, Op. 65 – Jean L. Kreiling
- Prelude in C Major, Op. 28, No. 1 – Maja Trochimczyk
- Prelude in A Minor, Op. 28, No. 2 – Leonard Kress
- Prelude in E Minor, Op. 28, No. 4 – illustration by Sigismond Ivanowski
- Prelude in C-sharp Minor, Op. 28, No. 10 – illustration by Sigismond Ivanowski
- Prelude in D-flat Major, Op. 28, No. 15 ("Raindrop Prelude") – Donna L. Emerson, Christine Klocek-Lim, Richard Pflum, Carrie A. Purcell, Cheryl M. Thatt
- Prelude in C Minor, Op. 28, No. 20 – Donna L. Emerson
- Waltz in D-flat Major, Op. 64, No. 1 ("Minute Waltz") – Clark Crouch, Laura L. Mays Hoopes, Marlene Hitt, Ben Humphrey, Taoli-Ambika Talwar, Marianne Worthington
- Waltz in A-flat Major, Op. 69, No. 1 ("Farewell Waltz") – Millicent Borges Accardi, Kathi Stafford
- Waltz in A Minor, Op. Posthumous – Lois P. Jones, Charlotte Jones, Dean Pasch, Russell Salamon
- Other pieces without specific opus numbers: ballades, polonaises, scherzo

# Introduction: The Poetry of Chopin in Poetry

## Maja Trochimczyk

1.

The *Chopin with Cherries* anthology celebrates the 200th birth anniversary of Polish pianist-composer Fryderyk Chopin (1810-1849) in a gathering of over 120 English-language poems. Ninety-two poets are represented here. Four "classics" span the late 19th and early 20th centuries: Cyprian Kamil Norwid, Emma Lazarus, Amy Lowell and T. S. Eliot. The anthology includes one important Polish romantic poem, Cyprian Kamil Norwid's *Fortepian Szopena*, in a new English translation by Leonard Kress. While it is the first extensive survey of Chopin-themed poetry in English, presenting nearly 100 original, newly written works, *Chopin with Cherries* has several predecessors that deserve a mention. John Minczeski's anthology of Polish American writings, including prose and poetry by 23 authors, takes its title from a poem by Margaret C. Szumowski, *Concert at Chopin's House* (1988).[1] This poem, portraying life in Poland behind the Iron Curtain, is reprinted in the present anthology. In 1993, a Canadian poet Marilyn Bowering wrote a poetic account of the love affair between Chopin and George Sand, entitling her 97-page volume *Love as it is*.[2] Books of poetry with Chopin in the title include *Chopin and other Poems* by Jocelyn Hollis (1972), and a chapbook published in 2005 by Mark Tardi, called *First Part—Chopin's Feet*.[3] Hollis's is a collection of traditional verse, whereas Tardi's inspiration may be found among the avant-garde, especially poets of the surreal. *Chopin's Piano*—besides being immortalized in Cyprian Kamil Norwid's *Fortepian Szopena*—is the title of a poetry collection by Charles Adés Fishman (2006).

Collecting poetry about music seems to be quite fashionable these days. *The Music Lover's Poetry Anthology* of over 150 poems about music was edited by poet Helen Handley Houghton and pianist Maureen McCarthy Draper in 2007.[4] The collection includes classics from Sappho and Rumi, through Baudelaire and Neruda, to contemporary poets like Adam Zagajewski, Robert Pinsky and Adrienne Rich. The sections deal with listening, composers, genres, various instruments and the music of nature. Another recently issued anthology *Music's Spell: Poems About Music and Musicians* was edited by Emily Fragos for Random House (2009). With over 160 poems from the antiquity to the present, the anthology's highlights the topics of the power of music, love, instruments, voice, composers, individual pieces, lessons and learning, pop/rock and jazz/blues. For her anthology, Fragos selected a fragment from Amy Lowell's "Chopin" and recommended the inclusion of this delightful poem in the present collection.

*Chopin with Cherries* brings together a variety of approaches and poetic forms, including free verse, letters, stanzaic poems, prose poetry, villanelle, sonnet, and tanka. Some poets write about details from Chopin's life: his loves, Maria Wodzińska (1819-1896) and George Sand (1804-1876),[5] or the circumstances of his illness and death. Others focus on his music—on its meaning as a symbol of fragile beauty in the modern world, or on the emotional and aesthetic impact of individual pieces. What are the poems about? Let's summarize the topics: Chopin (238), of course, but also love (82), music (80), playing (79) the notes (70), light (71) and life (40). In Chopin's world according to American poets, the playing of music brings love to mind and the night (41) is filled with song (20). Here, it is evening (41) far more often than morning (10); the preferred seasons are the fall and the summer. It may rain (25) or snow (12); but it is all new (81) under the sun (14) and the moon (12). Light (71) brightens up the sky (21); it is sometimes dark (22) when shadows (14) spread amidst clouds (11). The artificial world's color scheme differs from the black and white keyboard in its bluish tinge, established by the predominant colors: white – 30, blue – 22, black – 12, and red – 12, followed by gold – 5, green – 4, yellow – 4, silver – 3, and grey – 3. There is much to treasure (4): pearls (4), diamonds (3), even rubies (3) and sapphires (2). Love (82) triumphs over death (18).

2.

Of the 92 poets whose work is gathered in this volume, five are no longer with us (Norwid, Lazarus, Lowell, T.S. Eliot and

William Pillin). Their classic works bring an abundance of ideas and tropes to the subject: the meaning and place of art in society; and the experiential, sensual and spiritual content of artworks. Among contemporary poets, fifteen have contributed two poems each (for a total of 30 poems) and seven poets have written three poems each. In many cases, poets write about similar topics, as if trying to find their perfect expression: Taoli-Ambika Talwar is fascinated with waltzes, Katrin Talbot with mazurkas, while Ryan McLellan reflects on listening to the radio or recordings. With 51 poems penned by 23 poets, the collection's diversity is assured by the remaining 69 poets, from classics to recent graduates, each represented by one work. The full list of 92 names is in the contributors' section including short biographical information.

A review of these biographies reveals the richness of experience accumulated by contemporary English-language poets interested in Chopin's life and music. They have published several hundreds of books and thousands of poems. Their backgrounds span the twin categories commonly distinguished (and often diametrically opposed) as "academic" and "community" poetry. The anthology unites them in a single purpose: expressing the intangible experience of music as heard, played, and remembered. The only criterion for inclusion was the editor's preference. *Chopin with Cherries*, named after one of my own poems, is a tribute to the great composer, whose music haunted my Polish childhood. After being invited to the 2010 International Chopin Congress in Warsaw (the third such momentous event, following the congresses in 1949 and 1999 that celebrated Chopin's death anniversaries),[6] I decided to gather and analyze English-language poetry about Chopin as an original contribution to the scholarly proceedings. From these modest beginnings, the book grew until its scope and quality vastly exceeded my expectations. For this, I owe a debt of gratitude to the poets and their immense love of Chopin.

Who are, then, the 92 musical poets? Native speakers, second and first generation immigrants, they reside in the U.S., Canada (Helen Vandepeer), England (Lia Brooks and Anna Maria Mickiewicz), Germany (Dean Pasch), Mexico (Allison Campbell), the Philippines (Maxine R. Syjuco), and Poland (an American expatriate, Mark Tardi). The first generation immigrants came to America from Australia (Katrin Talbot and Helen Vandepeer),

Austria (Erika Wilk), India (Taoli-Ambika Talwar), the Philippines (R. Romea Luminarias), Poland (Beata Poźniak Daniels, Oriana Ivy, and Maja Trochimczyk), and Serbia (Mira N. Mataric). The countries of origin of the second generation, whose parents crossed the ocean, include the Czech Republic (Radomir Vojtech Luza), Malta (Kath Abela Wilson), and Poland (John Z. Guzlowski and Elisabeth Murawski). Some poets live on farms in Canada, others in American college towns, and still others hail from metropolitan centers in Europe (London) and America (New York, Los Angeles, and Seattle). About thirty poets have held or currently hold academic appointments at such diverse institutions as Arizona State University, Bridgewater State College in Massachusetts, Columbia University, College of the Desert in California, Minnesota State University Moorhead, Mount Ida College, New Mexico State University, Owens College, Rainier Writers' Workshop, San Jose State University, University of Łódź in Poland, and Widener University. A sizeable group has recently retired from academic appointments, but continues writing poetry (Victor Contoski, Charles Adés Fishman, John Z. Guzlowski, Ben Humphrey, Niels Peterson, and Marian Kaplun Shapiro). There are several recent graduates of creative writing programs, with MFAs and Ph.D.s. Many poets and writers pursue double careers, often in the healing professions (doctors, psychologists, and social workers).

The range of their accomplishments is impressive, with a vast array of national and international residences, fellowships, and awards to their credit. Nine poets received, between them, 25 Pushcart Prize nominations given for the best poem published in a journal. Four poet-laureates uphold this ancient tradition in Alameda, CA (Mary Rudge), Massachusetts (Marian Kaplun Shapiro), Santa Clara County, CA (Nils Peterson), and Sunland-Tujunga, a suburb of Los Angeles (Marlene Hitt). There are poets-painters, artists, or photographers (Lia Brooks, Kerri Buckley, Maxine R. Syjuco, Taoli-Ambika Talwar, and Maja Trochimczyk). Others are performance artists, pianists, actors, or singers (Beata Poźniak Daniels, Fiona Sze-Lorrain, Maxine R. Syjuco, Ryan McLellan, and Gabriel Shanks).

Many poets are involved in arts non-profits, organizing poetry reading series, workshops, and other events. The largest group consists of editors and publishers. Some of them manage small presses: Charlie Durrant at PIGGY INK, Roxanne Hoffman at Poets Wear Prada, Jeffrey Levine at Tupelo Press, Lois P. Jones at Word Walker Press, Rick Lupert at Poetry Super Highway, Fiona Sze-Lorrain at Cerise Press, the editor (yours truly) at Moonrise Press, and Kath Abela Wilson at Poets on Site in Pasadena. Other poets serve as editors and publishers of a multitude of poetry journals, to mention only the *Aufgabe* (Mark Tardi), *Autumn Sky Poetry* (Christine Klocek-Lim), *California Quarterly* (Russell Salamon), *Clockwise Cat* (Alison Ross), *Kyoto Journal* (Lois P. Jones), *poeticdiversity* (Marie Lecrivain), and *Naugatuck River Review* (Lori Desrosiers).

3.

The association of Chopin's music with poetry dates back to his Parisian concerts reviewed by German expatriate poet, Heinrich Heine. On 4 February 1937, Heine published an essay in the *Revue et Gazette Musicale* stating of Chopin: "He is a poet of sound."[7] Again, in *Lutetia*, a collection of his Parisian reviews published in 1855, Heine wrote that Chopin

> *is much more a composer than a virtuoso. In the case of Chopin, I completely forget the mastery of piano-playing, and sink into the sweet abysses of his music, into the painful sweetness of his equally deep and tender creations. Chopin is the great genius tone-poet.*[8]

Heine continued to define Chopin's art as poetry elsewhere:

> *Yes, we must attribute genius to Chopin in the full sense of the word: he is not merely a virtuoso, he is also a poet, he can bring to our intuition the poetry that lives in his soul, he is a tone poet, and nothing equals the pleasure he creates for us when he sits at the piano and improvises ... his true fatherland is the dream realm of poetry.*[9]

Thus, a poet found Chopin to be also a poet, a "universal artist." This affinity was confirmed by a virtuoso pianist composer, Franz Liszt (1811-1886), a Chopin contemporary, sometime friend and rival. Liszt established the *topos* of Chopin's art as pure poetry in a biography published soon after Chopin's death (1852), first as a series of articles in *La France musicale*.[10] In this text, named simply after the composer, Liszt stated that the Polish master "moved among us like a spirit consecrated by all that Poland possesses of poetry."[11] He also found Chopin's flowing, irregular rhythms, known as *tempo rubato*, to be particularly poetic. The highly popular biography was co-authored by Liszt's mistress, a prolific writer, Princess Carolyne zu Sayn-Wittgenstein.[12] Cast in an extravagantly florid language of the mid-19th century, the biography established and disseminated the poetic image of Chopin that captured the attention of numerous writers and painters.

Via several English-language editions of Liszt's biography and through the efforts of its American translator, Martha Walker Cook (1807-1874), the image of Chopin as a poet of sound entered American letters.[13] Her translation of Liszt's biography, dedicated to a forgotten Polish émigré pianist Jan N. Pychowski (1818-1900), was first published in 1863 and by 1880 reached its fourth edition.[14]

American poet Emma Lazarus (1849-1887), knew this book well, as she knew and loved Chopin's music.[15] Her long poem established a conceptual sphere in which to view Chopin's oeuvre: a world of exalted spirituality, rich symbolism, subtle elegance, angelic sensitivity, and aristocratic sophistication. For instance, Jeffrey Kallberg's study of gender issues in Chopin reception borrows Lazarus's phrases to capture the "effeminate" image of the composer.[16] The four-stanza poem about the great composer, known for his perfectionist polishing of his musical gems, consists of four sonnets, each with a different variant of the rhyme scheme:

|      |                      |
| ---- | -------------------- |
| I.   | a b a b  c d c d  e f e f g g |
| II.  | a b b a  c d d c  e e f e e f |
| III. | a b a b  c d c d  e f e f g g |
| IV.  | a b a b  c d c d  e f f e g g |

Stanzas I and II are in the form of the English sonnet; stanza IV is its variant and stanza II has elements from an Italian sonnet, with its characteristic avoidance of the final, rhymed couplet. The long, ten-syllable lines flow smoothly, with rich imagery. For Lazarus, in Chopin's music,

*... beneath the strain*
*Of reckless revelry, vibrates and sobs*

> *One fundamental chord of constant pain,*
> *The pulse-beat of the poet's heart that throbs.*
> ...
>
> *The Polish poet who sleeps silenced long,*
> *The seraph-souled musician, breathes again*
> *Eternal eloquence, immortal pain.*

The matter was set, then. Chopin was a poet of a very peculiar kind: "The poet who must sound earth, heaven, and hell!" (Lazarus). In attempting to thus define the poetic task of music, Lazarus had unknowingly followed in the footsteps of Polish romantic poet, Cyprian Kamil Norwid (1821-1883), who, in his masterly poem about Chopin's piano, *Fortepian Szopena,* articulated the timelessness of perfection found in Chopin's works, contrasted with the violent destruction of his instrument by the Russian soldiers: "Behold – how noble thought / Is trampled by human fury." Norwid's classic verse was deemed too difficult to translate by Adam Czerniawski for his earlier English-language edition.[17] American poet Leonard Kress rose to the occasion and rendered the poet's obscure metaphors in splendid English.

The destruction of Chopin's piano occurred during one of the battles in the tumultuous period after the January Uprising in 1863, when Russian soldiers ravaged a Warsaw palace where the piano was housed and threw the historic instrument out of the window. This moment became a symbol of savage destruction of beauty by violence and appears in three other poems in this volume, by Kerri Buckley, Charles Adés Fishman and Leonard Kress. Fishman's poem is reprinted from his book *Chopin's Piano* (2006), exploring humanity's brutality, witnessed in the iconoclastic act of the Russian soldiers, as well as in "the expulsion of the Jews from Spain, the death of Lorca, and violence in the Holy Land."

The association of Chopin's music with the heights of poetic achievement coupled with spiritual enlightenment remained a fertile strand in English-language writings about Chopin. In 1902, Fanny Morris Smith published an essay attempting to answer the question, "What poet is most akin to Chopin?" in response to what she considered an erroneous suggestion that Lord Tennyson was Chopin's spiritual brother.[18] No, said Ms. Smith, John Keats was the exact poetic match for the composer-pianist.

Even posing such a question seems ridiculously archaic in the 21$^{st}$ century; yet the search for the "poetic" in Chopin's music persists, with numerous poets dedicating their work to the "eternal eloquence, immortal pain" (phrases from Emma Lazarus) or "nothing but moonlight" in Chopin's music. The latter phrase emerged in George Sand's account of a conversation between Chopin and Delacroix, and was, according to Sand, actually uttered by the composer when pondering the relative importance of color and shape in a work of art. Chopin said, "What if I find nothing but moonlight?" To this, Delacroix responded, "Then you will have found the reflection of a reflection." Sand commented on this exchange by describing the scenery: "Suddenly the note of blue sings out, and the night is all around us, azure and transparent. Light clouds take on fantastic shapes and fill the sky."[19] This poetic scene inspired Susan Rogers to include it as an epigraph, accompanied by a photograph of the moon as integral parts of her poem, "Alicia Plays Chopin." Millicent Borges Accardi used the same quotation differently:

> *Uncertain is the shape / of romance*
> *Sketching and observation / Finds / nothing but moonlight.*
> *Mediterranean and dawn are / melodies / written from life.*

By the time of the early 20$^{th}$-century modernists, T. S. Eliot in England and Amy Lowell in the U.S., who wrote about Chopin in the second decade of the century, the music of this composer assumed two primary literary associations: first, with various aspects of romance, where the music was linked to the feminine beauty and sophistication (T.S. Eliot's "Portrait of a Lady"), and, second, with the timeless perfection of artistic achievement, contrasted with the brevity and frailty of human life, a sentiment captured in the classic phrase, *ars longa, vita brevis* (Lowell's "Chopin").

While describing Chopin's suffering in graphic terms of "blood on the keyboard," Lowell's poem touched upon the third important trope in the poetic reception of this composer—that of death, mortality and morbidity. This thematic cluster was associated with Chopin especially strongly at the end of the 19$^{th}$ century and through the early decades of the 20$^{th}$ century.[20] His illness and death exerted an eerie fascination upon artists and poets. A life cut short in his 39th year, a creative talent destroyed by an incurable illness, the most romantic of maladies, the "consumption"—all these elements featured prominently in the poetic and artistic responses to his music.[21] It is important to point out that this literary trope of mortality/morbidity as a primary association with Chopin was established through Liszt's detailed narrative of the last days and hours of the dying pianist. Many other essayists and writers, including Stanisław Przybyszewski (1868-1927), sought to identify the spiritual quality of art created at the threshold of death. Przybyszewski and Polish composer Zygmunt Noskowski (1846-1909) elaborated on the topic of the "typically Slavic" feeling of the unspecific, yet overwhelming, "sorrow" ("żal" or "żałość") and nostalgia permeating Chopin's music.[22] This overriding expressive tone was associated with a general poetic quality in Noskowski's 1899 article, "The Essence of Chopin's Works:"

> *Whatever we call the mood in Chopin's works, be it "elegiac quality," "longing," or "sorrowfulness," it is of primary importance to state that, above all, the purest poetry prevails in them and that the breath of this poetry captures the hearts in a way that cannot be described with words.*[23]

I illustrate the widespread focus on sorrow, death and skeletal visions by reproducing 19th century postcards, associated with the forms of the nocturne and the funeral march. These artistic interpretations of sounds as images often breach the limits of what is considered truly artistic, reaching into the domain of kitsch. Luckily, a similar accusation cannot be addressed at Lowell. In her "Chopin" poem, the lyrical subject, while speaking to her cat, Winky, contrasts her own creative malaise with the scope of Chopin's achievements. His oeuvre is all the more impressive, when she remembers that he created these musical treasures while being mortally ill with tuberculosis. The poem is divided into three parts and framed by the heroine talking to Winky about the cat's failure to catch mice, which is equal to the author's failure to write, in contrast with the dying Chopin, the focus of the central part. He struggled with mortal illness while working on his sublime creations: "Music drenched in blood, / Flights of arpeggios confused by blood." She concludes: "He bore it." She should also try to endure, fighting her own obstacles, however smallish.

Postcard *Chopin's Vision*, based on a painting by T. Korpal, *Wizya Chopina*. Kraków: Wydawnictwo Salonu Malarzy Polskich, ca. 1900-1910. Maja Trochimczyk Collection.

The topic of Chopin's incurable consumption is mentioned in several new poems seeking to capture the essence of his life at its key creative and dramatic moments (Donna L. Emerson, Laura L. Mays Hoopes, Christine Klocek-Lim, and William Pillin). The themes of death and dying are taken up by many contemporary poets: George Bodmer, Jennifer S. Flescher, Jarek Gajewski, Radomir Luza, Elisabeth Murawski, Kenneth Pobo, Fiona Sze-Lorrain, Erika Wilk, and Anne Harding Woodworth. Other poets reflect on Chopin's last words (Flescher), his final hour (Woodworth), his death mask (Sze-Lorrain), the lock of his hair in the museum (Murawski), the burial of his heart in Warsaw and his body in Paris (Wilk), and the strange intensity of contemporaneous accounts of his agony (Bodmer). Shayla Hawkins heard in the Funeral March "Chopin's fingers / on the piano /strong as a gravedigger's hands." She had a predecessor, Henry Grafton Chapman who, in 1906, self-published *Words for Chopin's Funeral March*.[24] Poets associate Chopin's death with the genre of the nocturne (Jarek Gajewski); or compare the brevity of his life to the Minute Waltz (Laura L. Mays Hoopes and Marlene Hitt).

T. S. Eliot's classic portrait of a romantic discord ushers in the modernist era; ironic and wry, it marks the demise of overwrought romanticism. After hearing "the latest Pole, transmit the Preludes by his hair and finger-tips" (this is an allusion to the golden halo of hair of the "archangel of the piano," Ignacy Jan Paderewski),[25] the elegant and sophisticated lady comments about the subtle quality of Chopin's music:

> *"So intimate, this Chopin, that I think his soul*
> *Should be resurrected only among friends*
> *Some two or three, who will not touch the bloom*
> *That is rubbed and questioned in the concert room."*

The self-centered, overly talkative heroine chatters about her experiences and ideas in a way that is immensely irritating to her listener, a caddish man who has other things on his mind and longs for his sports and comics. Eliot's "portrait" is a classic expression of modernist detachment, a favorite of literary critics and historians.[26] From our vantage point, though it is more important that by associating "the seraph-winged" Chopin with the Lady's fanciful ideas, Eliot connected his music to the male-female relationships, love affairs, and spurious heartbreaks. In this, he paved the way for a distinct strand in Chopin reception by contemporary poets.

Love—experienced, cherished, imagined, rejected and remembered—is the predominant topic associated with Chopin's works by American poets. In contrast, according to musicologist Halina Goldberg, Poles tended to see the music as portrayals of the native country, or expressions of the composer's patriotic and "prophetic voice."[27] Some poets use the music as a backdrop for their intense, sensuous feelings (Marie Lecrivain and R. Romea Luminarias). Others focus on the quiet joys of domestic bliss (Helen Vandepeer) or the loss of love remembered through music (Lucy Anderton, Charlie Durrant, and Dean Pasch). The transformation of romantic affection into the love of music itself and the transcendence of suffering through art are themes embraced by Taoli-Ambika Talwar and Kath Abela Wilson. Still others envision love as inhabiting the music, especially the nocturnes (Victor Contoski, Lola Haskins, and Leonore Wilson).

In Lola Haskins's evocative nocturne, "A warm wind splits the song / into two streams of birds." William Pillin's "ineffable nocturnes / float away like farewell whispers." In Lia Brooks's interpretation, the music "expands outward in waves, measured / like tide, new moons, measured like the years in wood." The nocturne reminds Leonore Wilson about her mother's knowledge of "the smell of jasmine and mint, / the budding sound of a chrysalis." Russell Salamon speaks of "harvested wheat, fresh bread" as he also envisions "black butterflies whose shadowy / rhythms weep for a form." Written in 2009, his images of wheat and bread are a poetic response to my "Harvesting Chopin" with "the freshly-baked rye bread / sweetened by the strands / of music." There are many other poetic dialogues, scattered throughout, as poets speak to Chopin, cite his Stuttgart Diaries and letters, quote his contemporaries, and allude to each other's work.

Chopin's love life is of particular interest to poets, obsessed with his relationship with George Sand (Austin Alexis, Sheila Black, Sharon Chmielarz, Jessica Day, Lori Desrosiers, Donna L. Emerson, Gretchen Fletcher, Helen Graziano, Roxanne Hoffman, Carol J. Jennings, Georgia Jones-Davis, Elisabeth Murawski, Susan Rogers, Kathi Stafford, Erika Wilk, Martin Willitts Jr., and Meg Withers). Poets ponder the nature of that passionate, yet doomed relationship, especially during its last, discordant phase. They cite expressions from the couple's letters: Sand's "beloved little corpse" (Chmielarz and Willitts Jr.) and Chopin's "I tell my piano the things I used to tell you" (Roxanne Hoffman and Jessica Day). In contrast, the ambitious debutante, Maria Wodzińska, who spurned the pianist's advances, attracts far less attention, featuring in only five poems (Beata Poźniak Daniels, Kathi Stafford, and Tammy L. Tillotson). The form of an epistolary poem often occurs in this context. In three imaginary letters to and from Chopin, Tammy L. Tillotson tries to capture Chopin's heartbreak in the 1830s, marked by a packet of letters, that he had tied with a ribbon and inscribed "moja bieda" ("my misery"). Similarly, through epistolary poems, Martin Willitts Jr. recreates the growing discord between Chopin and Sand after their romance fell apart and the sick pianist was close to death in 1847. Taking the cue from the composer's notebooks, Roxanne Hoffman entitles her letter-poem, "G" for George and signs it "F" for Frédéric. Carol Jennings sends a love letter back in time to Chopin himself, thinking of all the loving dedications to ladies that crowd the first pages of his scores.

Beyond love affairs, two life-changing events from Chopin's biography act as magnets for the poets' imagination: his departure from Poland on the brink of the November Uprising of 1830 (Jeffrey Levine, Laura L. Mays Hoopes, and Elisabeth Murawski), and his ill-fated stay at a rainy and cold monastery at Valldemossa, Mallorca (Majorca), marking a time of illness and personal crisis (Christine Klocek-Lim, Lusia Slomkowska and Erika Wilk). Mentions of Mallorca/Majorca also appear in poems by Jeffrey Levine, Donna L. Emerson, Carrie A. Purcell, and William Pillin. Finally, some poets, most notably, Levine, O'Hara and Pillin, give us vivid vignettes of the main events in Chopin's life, seeking to capture the essence of his creativity.

The choice of musical inspirations is interesting: many poets write about preludes (20), nocturnes (16), waltzes (14) and mazurkas (13). Other works attract far less attention. The genre of the etude merits nine mentions, the ballade – five, the polonaise – five, the sonata – five, the concerto, scherzo and *Fantasie Impromptu* – two each. *Berceuse* appears in poetry only once. Nocturnes are particularly popular as a genre, with 16 poems, associating the music with a full range of concepts from romance, to timeless beauty, to death. Some poets try to capture the meaning of an entire genre: all the preludes (Nils Petersen), nineteen waltzes (Emily Fragos), or ballades heard at different historical times (Gretchen Fletcher). Others mention an array of musical forms, each endowed with a different expressive character (Marian Kaplun Shapiro, Leonore Wilson, and Kerri Buckley).

To give justice to the musical genres that became focal points of poetic inspiration, I divided the volume into fourteen sections consisting of poems on the same or related theme: Chopin's name, piano, his preludes, etudes, mazurkas, polonaises, waltzes, nocturnes, other pieces, his life, his death, listening and playing his music, and its beauty in general. This classification is arbitrary since many themes may be interwoven in a counterpoint of ideas in one particular poem.

Four miniatures proved to be the most inspiring: the Waltz in D-flat Major, Op. 64, No. 1 "Minute Waltz" (six poems, including a cowboys' dance by Clark Crouch, and verse by Laura L. Mays Hoopes, Marlene Hitt, Ben Humphrey, Taoli-Ambika Talwar, and Marianne Worthington), the Prelude in D-flat Major, Op. 28, No. 15 "Raindrop" (five poems by Donna L. Emerson, Christine Klocek-Lim, Richard Pflum, Carrie A. Purcell, and Cheryl M. Thatt), the Waltz in A Minor, Op. Posthumous (four poems by Lois P. Jones, Charlotte Jones, Dean Pasch, and Russell Salamon), and Nocturne in E-flat Major, Op. 9, No. 2 (three poems by Carol J. Jennings, Marie Lecrivain, and Linda Nemec Foster).

Chopin is heard everywhere: in a Parisian church (Rick Lupert), on the plains of North Dakota (Thom Tammaro), in Ohio (Donna L. Emerson), while driving to Palm Springs (Ruth Nolan), in the wind blowing across the deserts of New Mexico (Joseph Somoza), on the radio (Ryan McLellan, Maja Trochimczyk), on the plane to Seattle (Peggy Castro), at home while watching a snowfall dance to the music (Helen Vandepeer), or while listening to live performance by an old auntie (Marlene Hitt), mother (Lia Brooks, Gabriel Shanks, and Leonore Wilson), daughter (Mira N. Mataric), or tragically lost sister (Charlotte Jones). Finally, Elizabyth Hiscox hears Chopin among the stars, dedicating her poem to "3784 Chopin – small asteroid in main belt."

Mary Rudge and Devi Walders describe the transformation of music into dance by Isadora Duncan (1877-1927) and Alexandra Ansanelli (b. 1981). In the words of Walders, while attending a farewell performance of the young ballerina, "we watch this last poetry of movement / as each musical gesture becomes a dance gesture." Dance also permeates poems by Kerri Buckley, Lori Desrosiers, Victor Contoski, Russell Salamon, and Mira N. Mataric. The "Waltzes" section is particularly dance-like. Lori Desrosiers charms us with a waltz in words, by carefully maintaining the "ONE-two-three" rhythm, spinning the dancers around the room and the words throughout her poem. Taoli-Ambika Talwar creates a delicate line of words to last—when read aloud—as long as the waltz she portrays, about one minute.

The issue of Chopin's relationship to Poland recurs frequently. Millicent Borges Accardi declares triumphantly that Chopin is "more Polish than Poland." Others speak about his suffering and sorrow (Emma Lazarus, Georgia Jones-Davis, William Pillin, and Jeffrey Levine, to mention just a couple examples), or his ability to transform Polish folk music into classical gems admired by the whole world. The latter trope has roots (or parallels) in Norwid's classic verse.

Several Polish American poets (of the ten included in *Chopin with Cherries*)[28] write about listening to Chopin in Poland. John Z. Guzlowski considers echoes of the war in polonaises heard by his father ("A Good Death"). He hopes that, in time, the music would replace traumatic memories of "the hollow surge and dust of German tanks." Margaret C. Szumowski's "Concert at Chopin's House" depicts, in a nutshell, the entire country under communist oppression: a troubled, challenging life that overflows with music at Żelazowa Wola, Chopin's birthplace. Sharon Chmielarz thinks of a concert heard during her visit to Kraków, the ancient capital of the "old country." Linda Nemec Foster reflects on nostalgia and the ugliness of the Mazovian willows, crooked trees planted along the fields of Chopin's childhood and often featured in his iconography. Oriana Ivy remembers the Chopin monument in Warsaw as a sign of her spiritual and artistic home that she left at 17.

While many poets wrote about Chopin's Polishness and his attachment to the country of his origins (Millicent Borges Accardi, Elisabeth Murawski, William Pillin and Erika Wilk are great examples), only Polish-Americans intimately shared his longing for the lost homeland. That imaginary realm, more often than not, was a site of an innocent, blissful childhood (Marlene Hitt, Donna L. Emerson, Taoli-Ambika Talwar, Maja Trochimczyk, Martin Willits Jr., and Leonore Wilson). Poets fondly remember listening to the music associated with their carefree youth, as the sounds evoke moments of past happiness. My poem "A Study with Cherries" that gave the title to this volume evokes the bittersweet tastes of my childhood: "a rich, sweet cherry" that sprinkles "its dark notes / on my skin, like rainy preludes / drizzling through the air" and the "white flesh" of a walnut, "a study in C Major." Two poems I based on mazurkas, "Harvesting Chopin" and "How to Make a Mazurka," are recollections of Chopin's music heard during daily broadcasts by the Polish Radio in the villages of my Polish and Belorussian grandparents, where I spent my summer vacations. In general, nostalgia and the longing for the forgotten or destroyed past finds an expression in a variety of poems gathered in the volume, to cite only the description of a blighted neighborhood revisited by Marianne Worthington.

Several poets mention specific pianists who inspired them: Ryszard Bakst (Anna Maria Mickiewicz), Artur Rubinstein (Donna L. Emerson), Leon Fleisher (David Ellis), Mario Feninger (Lois P. Jones), Jean Yves Thibaudet (Cheryl M. Thatt), and Emmanuel Ax in Piano Concerto No. 2 in F Minor (Katrin Talbot),. Yet many of them, as listeners, would agree with Witold Gombrowicz's remark cited by Mark Tardi: "I much prefer the Chopin that reaches me in the street from an open window to the Chopin served in great style from the concert stage."

Listening to the music played by someone else, in the concert hall, in the street, or on the radio, is the most frequent type of a musical-poetic experience. Some poets' affection for Chopin's music is revealed in their biographic notes at the end of the book. Georgia Jones-Davis's note is particularly vivid in this respect: "That she began, whilst a student, to compose poetry at the same time that she started to listen to the music of Chopin is no coincidence, she insists." Accounts of Chopin "as heard" include numerous poems in addition to the fourteen works grouped together in the "Listening" section of the anthology.

It is the consolation of the music that elicits the most startling responses of poetic imagination. In the words of Lois P. Jones, writing about Chopin's waltz:

> *Melody circles like a falcon in your parlor,*
> *as if a note were a bird charmer who knows*
> *my thoughts by name.*

Metaphors bring together other sounds: birdsong (Lola Haskins, William Pillin, Richard Pflum), wind chimes (Marlene Hitt) and the wind (Ben Humphrey, Linda Nemec Foster, Joseph Somoza, and Taoli-Ambika Talwar). The sweet taste of juicy fruit is savored with the music, to mention only the cherries of the title, Mirabelle plums tasted by Lois P. Jones, and peaches remembered by Diane Shipley DeCillis and Emily Fragos, ("19 Waltzes"). Mira N. Mataric recalls the flavor of berries and apples; the latter may also be found "rolling over cobbles" in Sharon Chmielarz's fascinating take on impermanence. The poets' synaesthesic approach associates the music with a multitude of colors, images, tastes, textures, and feelings (Kerrie Buckley, Emily Fragos, Lola Haskins, and Leonore Wilson, among others). Whole worlds are discovered when the music is heard.

Playing the music has also proven to have an intense inspirational power, as shown in nine poems dedicated specifically to this topic and many others scattered throughout the book. Poets remember learning the music in childhood, being frustrated by its difficulties or elated by the beauty. Many of them reveal a profound attachment to Chopin's music, acquired through learning how to play the piano. We should note that there are several music professionals among the poets (Jean L. Kreiling—a music historian specializing in interdisciplinary studies of music and poetry; Rick Lupert—a music teacher; Ryan McLellan—a singer and song writer; Fiona Sze-Lorrain—a classical pianist and performer on the Chinese gushing; and the editor, a musicologist). There are also several performance artists and actors, accustomed to the stage (Beata Poźniak Daniels, Maxine R. Syjuco and Gabriel Shanks).

Chopin's level of artistic sophistication inspired artists to experiment with forms and images. Poetic forms include a sonnet (Jean L. Kreiling), villanelle (Kerri Buckley), tanka (Peggy Castro), and rhymed cowboy poetry (Clark Crouch). Poets organize their verse in numbered stanzas (Emma Lazarus, T. S. Eliot, Cyprian Kamil Norwid, Lola Haskins, Rosemary O'Hara, and Martin Willitts, Jr.). They separate sections by asterisks (Amy Lowell, William Pillin, Lia Brooks) or dates (Gretchen Fletcher). Poems are structured in couplets (Lucy Anderton, Kerri Buckley, Sharon Chmielarz, Jennifer S. Flescher, Lois P. Jones, Fiona Sze-Lorrain, Leonore Wilson and Marianne Worthington), tercets (Lia Brooks, David Ellis, Elisabeth Murawski, Lori Desrosiers, Shayla Hawkins, Kenneth Pobo, Joseph Somoza, and Anne Harding Woodworth), and quatrains (Clark Crouch, Taoli Ambika Talwar, and Maja Trochimczyk). I use a refrain in one of my mazurkas ("mix it – round and round to dizziness"), a recipe-poem stylized partly as a Polish folk-song and reflecting the sectional, repetitive form of Chopin's miniatures. Charles Adés Fishman's "Chopin's Piano" also circles around with a recurring thought: "we were not there to hear it." Of course, repetition is the very nature of the form of the villanelle, effectively used by Kerri Buckley.

Experiments abound, ranging from the surreal world of Alison Ross where "the stars drip melodies like blind pianos," through the mischief of Maxine R. Syjuco's who "ate Chopin," to the virtuosity of verbal associations in two poems by Radomir Vojtech Luza who eschews all upper-case letters and punctuation. Several poets play games with irregular indentation: Sharon Chmielarz, Victor Contoski, Ruth Nolan, and Meg Withers. Visual poetry is also created by careful placement of words on the page by Taoli-Ambika Talwar and Mark Tardi.

4.

Garrison Keillor, host of the *Prairie Home Companion*, wrote in "The Heart of Saturday Night" (2009):

> ...*The plane falls, the company slides, the good man is gone, the lawn turns brown, but with Chopin you come back to basics: Do I regret this life? Is it, despite all our brave words, a cheat and a waste? Does it make any slight difference to the universe that we are present?*[29]

In his evocative essay, Keillor captured an important idea associated with Chopin's music – that of "timeless beauty" – and "art as the meaning of life." He had heard it in an impromptu performance at a Saturday party, when a young girl suddenly sat down at the piano and played Chopin's Prelude in A Minor, thus transforming the evening into an encounter with transcendence.

Writing in a similar vein, many poets seek to express the intangible, yet profoundly moving impact of Chopin's music. Marian Kaplun Shapiro considers the meaning of Chopin's art "as if each measure were a casual ripple in a spring stream of melting centuries." She links its contemplative quality to the well-known Zen maxim about living immersed in the present: "eat when hungry / sleep when tired." The domestic bliss of living with the music inhabits also the work of Katrin Talbot ("Sewing with Chopin") and Ryan McLellan ("Artsy Evening"). Talbot envisions Chopin's music as a catalyst for healing, as he speaks "so eloquently / of the advantages of / a delicate / life." Beauty may also be an accusation for our failures, as the music plaintively sings: "'Why didn't you. . . ? Why did you . . . ?'" For Marilyn Robertson, playing Chopin is like learning a new language. Jeffrey Levine sees "scales scattered / like dried sea grass in the tidal pools." Ruth Nolan hears Chopin in the desert, "between the spaces of darkness and sound, blown across the sand dunes into magnificence." William Pillin hears "the ineffable nocturnes / float away like farewell whispers."

Poets continue to count their musical blessings and wonder about the mystery of Chopin's music that touches them so deeply. The last poem in *Chopin with Cherries*, Emily Fragos's "Chopiniana," expresses this feeling succinctly:

> *What remains moves fathomless and ravished, a Chopin of elation, performing so easily what is impossible to do.*

# ENDNOTES

[1] John Minczeski, ed., *Concert at Chopin's House* (New Rivers Press, 1988).
[2] Marilyn Bowering, *Love as it is*, Victoria, B.C. : Beach Holme Publishers, 1993.
[3] Jocelyn Hollis, *Chopin and Other Poems* (Fiddlehead Poetry Books, 1972); Mark Tardi, *Part First-----Chopin's Feet,* (g-o-n-g, 2005).
[4] Helen Handley Houghton and Maureen McCarthy Draper, eds., *The Music Lover's Poetry Anthology* (W. W. Norton & Co., 2007). Emily Fragos, *Music's Spell: Poems About Music and Musicians* (Random House, Inc., 2009).
[5] Sand was a pen name of Amantine (also "Amandine") Aurore Lucile Dupin, later Baroness (French: *baronne*) Dudevant.
[6] Irena Poniatowska, ed., *Chopin and His Work in the Context of Culture [Proceedings of the Second International Chopin Congress, October 1999]*. Kraków: Musica Iagellonica, 2003, 2 vols. My contribution was "From Art to Kitsch and Back Again? Chopin's Reception by Women Composers."
[7] Bernstein, Suzan, *Virtuosity of the Nineteenth Century: performing music and language in Heine, Liszt, and Baudelaire,* (Stanford University Press, 1998). Heine's statement is quoted from p. 77.
[8] Henrich Heine, *Sämtliche Werke*, vol. 5, SS 5: 442.
[9] Heine, *Sämtliche Werke*, Vol. 4: 278-279.
[10] Franz Liszt, *F. Chopin,* Nicole Priollaud, ed., reprint (Paris: L. Levy, 1990). English translation, *The Life of Chopin,* transl. Martha Walker Cook, first published in 1863, Project Gutenberg etext, infomotions.com/etexts/gutenberg/dirs/etext03/lfcpn10.htm
[11] Liszt, *The Life of Chopin,* trans. Martha Walker Cook, 1863, p. 44.
[12] See Charles Cooke, "Chopin and Liszt with a Ghostly Twist," *Notes,* Second Series, Vol. 22, No. 2 (Winter, 1965 - Winter, 1966), pp. 855-861. See also Irena Poniatowska, "The Polish Reception of Chopin Biography by Franz Liszt," in Halina Goldberg, ed., *The Age of Chopin,* op. cit., 259-276.

[13] Martha Walker Cook (1807-1874) published essays in the *Continental Monthly Magazine* and served for a time as its editor; in addition to translating Chopin's biography, she also translated works of Polish romantic literature including poetry by Zygmunt Krasiński.

[14] Cook considered Pychowski "a composer of true, deep, and highly original genius" but he is entirely forgotten by Polish music history. He is listed as "Bohemian" in the *New Grove Dictionary of Music and Musicians II* (2000).

[15] Gregory Eiselein, *Emma Lazarus: Selected Poems and Other Writings*, (Broadview Press, 2002); Esther Schor, *Emma Lazurus* (New York: Schocken, 2006).

[16] Jeffrey Kallberg, *Chopin at the Boundaries: Sex, History, and Musical Genre* (Cambridge, Mass.: Harvard University Press, 1996): "The Harmony of the Tea Table: Gender and Ideology in The Piano Nocturne" (pp. 30-61); "Small Fairy Voices: Sex, History, and Meaning in Chopin" (pp. 62-88).

[17] Cyprian Kamil Norwid, *Selected Poems*, trans. Adam Czerniawski (Anvil Press Poetry, 2004).

[18] Fanny Morris Smith, "What Poet is Most Akin to Chopin?" in Ignacy Jan Paderewski, et al., eds., *The Century Library of Music* (New York: The Century Magazine), vol. 18, p. 585ff.

[19] George Sand, *Impressions et Souvénirs* (Paris: Michel Lévy Frères, 1873).

[20] For period accounts about Chopin by 19th century Polish composers, including Zygmunt Noskowski, Ignacy Jan Paderewski, and Władysław Żeleński, see English translations of their writings gathered in an anthology edited by Maja Trochimczyk, *After Chopin: Essays in Polish Music* (USC, 2000).

[21] I discuss the topic of morbid/decadent vs. patriotic reception of Chopin in "Chopin and the 'Polish Race:' On National Ideologies and the Chopin Reception," in Halina Goldberg, ed. *The Age of Chopin* (Indiana University Press, 2004).

[22] Stanisław Przybyszewski, *Szopen a naród* (Kraków: Spółka Nakładowa Książka, ca. 1910s), and *Zur Psychologie des Individuums* (Berlin: Fontane, 1906). I present his views in the article on "Chopin and the Polish Race," in *The Age of Chopin,* op. cit.

[23] Zygmunt Noskowski, "The Essence of Chopin's Works," trans. By Maja Trochimczyk and in Maja Trochimczyk, ed., *After Chopin*, op. cit., 30.

[24] Only one copy of this book exists in the library of Brown University. Henry Grafton Chapman (1860-1913) was a poet, editor, and translator; he translated librettos of all major nineteenth century operas.

[25] This is an allusion to Polish pianist, Ignacy Jan Paderewski (1860-1941), famous for his golden-red halo of hair – an image widely disseminated and used in his publicity. See Maja Trochimczyk, "An Archangel at the Piano: Paderewski's Image and His Female Audience" (*Polish American Studies,* vol. 67, no. 1, Spring 2010).

[26] See George Williamson, "A Guide to Portrait of a Lady" in *The Griffin* 2, no. 3 ([March] 1953): 4-7; Jeffrey Wood, Lynn Wood, *Cambridge Critical Workshop,* Cambridge University Press, 2002; Derek Roper, "Eliot's 'Portrait of a Lady' restored," in *Essays in Criticism* 57 no. 1 (47-58).

[27] Halina Goldberg, "'Remembering that tale of grief:' The Prophetic Voice in Chopin's Music," in Halina Goldberg, ed., *The Age of Chopin*, op. cit., 54-94.

[28] The Polish-American poets are: Sharon Chmielarz, Victor Contoski, Linda Nemec Foster, John Z. Guzlowski, Oriana Ivy, Anna Maria Mickiewicz (she's actually Polish-English), Beata Poźniak, Lusia Slomkowska, Margaret C. Szumowski, and Maja Trochimczyk.

[29] Garrison Keillor, "The Heart of Saturday Night," *Salon.com,* June 3, 2009.

# Chopin with Cherries
# A Tribute in Verse

# Name

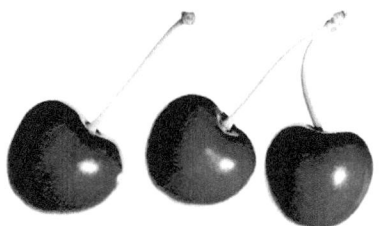

# Chopin

Emma Lazarus

I

A dream of interlinking hands, of feet
Tireless to spin the unseen, fairy woof
Of the entangling waltz. Bright eyebeams meet,
Gay laughter echoes from the vaulted roof.
Warm perfumes rise; the soft unflickering glow
Of branching lights sets off the changeful charms
Of glancing gems, rich stuffs, the dazzling snow
Of necks unkerchieft, and bare, clinging arms.
Hark to the music! How beneath the strain
Of reckless revelry, vibrates and sobs
One fundamental chord of constant pain,
The pulse-beat of the poet's heart that throbs.
So yearns, though all the dancing waves rejoice,
The troubled sea's disconsolate, deep voice.

II

Who shall proclaim the golden fable false
Of Orpheus' miracles? This subtle strain
Above our prose-world's sordid loss and gain
Lightly uplifts us. With the rhythmic waltz,
The lyric prelude, the nocturnal song
Of love and languor, varied visions rise,
That melt and blend to our enchanted eyes.
The Polish poet who sleeps silenced long,
The seraph-souled musician, breathes again
Eternal eloquence, immortal pain.
Revived the exalted face we know so well,
The illuminated eyes, the fragile frame,
Slowly consuming with its inward flame,
We stir not, speak not, lest we break the spell.

III

A voice was needed, sweet and true and fine
As the sad spirit of the evening breeze,
Throbbing with human passion, yet devine
As the wild bird's untutored melodies.
A voice for him 'neath twilight heavens dim,
Who mourneth for his dead, while round him fall
The wan and noiseless leaves. A voice for him
Who sees the first green sprout, who hears the call
Of the first robin on the first spring day.
A voice for all whom Fate hath set apart,
Who, still misprized, must perish by the way,
Longing with love, for that they lack the art
Of their own soul's expression. For all these
Sing the unspoken hope, the vague, sad reveries.


IV

Then Nature shaped a poet's heart--a lyre
From out whose chords the lightest breeze that blows
Drew trembling music, wakening sweet desire.
How shall she cherish him? Behold! she throws
This precious, fragile treasure in the whirl
Of seething passions; he is scourged and stung,
Must dive in storm-vext seas, if but one pearl
Of art or beauty therefrom may be wrung.
No pure-browed pensive nymph his Muse shall be,
An amazon of thought with sovereign eyes,
Whose kiss was poison, man-brained, worldy-wise,
Inspired that elfin, delicate harmony.
Rich gain for us! But with him is it well?
The poet who must sound earth, heaven, and hell!

# Chopin

Amy Lowell

The cat and I
Together in the sultry night
Waited.
He greatly desired a mouse;
I, an idea.
Neither ambition was gratified.
So we watched
In a still and painful expectation.
Little breezes pattered among the trees,
And thin stars ticked at us
Faintly,
Exhausted pulses
Squeezing through mist.

Those others, I said!
And my mind ran hollow as I tapped it.
Winky, I said,
Do all other cats catch the mice?

\*  \*  \*

It was low and long,
Ivory white with doors and windows blotting blue upon it.
Wind choked in pomegranate-trees,
Rain rattled on lead roofs,
And stuttered along twisted conduit-pipes.
An eagle screamed out of the heavy sky,
And some one in the house screamed,
"Ah, I knew that you were dead!"

So that was it:

Funeral chants
And the icy cowls of buried monks,
Organs on iron midnights,
And long wax winding sheets,
Guttered from altar candles.

First this,
Then spitting blood.
Music drenched in blood,
Flights of arpeggios confused by blood,
Flute showers of notes stung and arrested on a sharp chord,
Tangled in a web of blood.
"I cannot send you the manuscripts as they are not yet finished.
I have been ill as a dog.
My illness has had a pernicious effect on the Preludes
Which you will receive God knows when.

        \*        \*        \*

He bore it.
Therefore, Winky, drink some milk
And leave the mouse until to-morrow.
There are no blood-colored pomegranate flowers
Hurling their petals in at the open window,
But you can sit in my lap
And blink at a bunch of cinnamon-eyed coreopsis
While I pull your ears
In the manner which you find so infinitely agreeable.

# Chopin

William Pillin

Gautier wrote: "His soul weeps and hovers."
I prefer Nietzsche's "in him joy is ascendant."
It is easy to spit clichés at him:
effeminate, tearful, sylph-like . . .

"Sick-room poet" hissed envious Field,
ignoring the tough musical sinews,
the brooding rebellious rages
and the political passions.

True, his wit was exquisite and birdlike
but he knew how to summon the Furies
and spoke for his ravaged nation
in accents as daring as any.

He was elegant and consumptive.
He was successful in the world
and rejoiced over his triumphs.
He loved pretty women — and was loved by them.

\*

White and wasting he dotted
with splashes of blood his lunar pages,
carrying death like a singing bird
in his chest, his tissue held together

by dreams and bacilli. "I used to find him,"
wrote George Sand, "late at night at his piano,
pale, with haggard eyes, his hair almost standing,
and it was some minutes before he knew me."

In Majorca, the doctors
shuddered at his blood-flecked mouth,
burned his belongings, compelled him
to take refuge in a former monastery.

"My stone cell is shaped like a coffin.
You can roar — but always in silence."
When it stormed he wrote the 'raindrop' prelude
and from the thunder he fashioned an étude.

\*

"I work a lot," he wrote to his sister,
"I cross out all the time, I cough without measure."
With death's hand on his slender shoulder
he created ballades, études, nocturnes.

                      Who wrested
so much from torment?  Fading swiftly
he continued to color his silences,
a condemned man refusing a blindfold.

If he sometimes wept — it was from love, not weakness.
He felt all his life the wing of death's angel
brushing in their sleep the embracing lovers.
Can one truly sing without this terrible knowledge?

\*

Of the many men who were haunted
by the night, its gardens and fountains,
who fathomed it as truly as this Ariel of preludes?
The piano shakes like a leaf in the darkness.

The night breathes and triumphs.
Stars and sea-winds
drift through the open window.  The ineffable nocturnes
float away like farewell whispers.

Portrait of Chopin by Teofil Kwiatkowski (etching). reproduced in Frederick Niecks: *The Life of Chopin -Frederick Chopin As a Man and Musician* London and New York: Novello, Ewer & Co., 1888.

# Chopin

Millicent Borges Accardi

> *Into the wide world, with no very clearly defined aim, forever*
> —Jachimecki

One without
the other,
says Delacroix,
both will come together.

Find the mirror
of a mirror.

Wait for the sound
of a nightingale's full round
note.

A waltz in A-flat,
uncertain where the music
will settle
for good

A tormented heart,
one that dared not
inform him
no one else was listening.

Sonata,
mazurka, waltz, nocturne, étude,
impromptu and prélude—
the piano begins

Blue rings out
sounding in the ears,
cloud in his lungs.

Uncertain is the shape
of romance

Sketching and observation
finds
nothing but moonlight.

Mediterranean and dawn are
melodies
written from life.

# Chopin

## Alison Ross

the stars drip melodies
like blind pianos
tornados spin cacophonies
into a maze of violins

music is a labyrinth of tears
shed from the eyeless sun

# Chewing Chopin

Maxine R. Syjuco

He dined me with Chaucer and Chopin
not realizing, perchance, that Chopin
doesn't chew, doesn't spit,
doesn't gag, doesn't swallow,
doesn't move, doesn't chacha

Chopin doesn't like me—doesn't like you.

I hate Chopin.

Chopin hates me.

So I ate Chopin.

# Piano

# The Piano of Chopin

Cyprian Kamil Norwid

Translated by Leonard Kress

    1.

I was with you, almost to the end,
That impenetrable state –
Like myth – full
Like dawn – pale
When the end of life whispers to the beginning:
*I will not consume you…No…I come to consummate…*

    2.

I was with you those days, almost to the end,
When – each moment – you resembled more –
The lyre forsaken by Orpheus.
And with a song that tamed by the very strings,
Conversing with each other
And nudging themselves
In twos – in twos –
Murmuring out of the silence:
*…When did he begin
To strike those notes?
Is he such a Master…that he plays…
Though he spurns us?*

    3.

I was with you Frederyk in those days.
When the hand…possessed the whiteness
Of alabaster – and its manner and elegance,
Light and wavering like an ostrich plume,

Became confused in my eye
With the keyboard's ivory…
And you were like that figure sprung
From the womb of marble,
Formed only
By the chisel
Of genius – eternal Pygmalion.

    4.

But what you played – the tones you expressed – this will tell –
That more than echoes ornamenting,
Your hand alone was blessing
Each quivering chord…
Yet what you played – contained the simplicity
Of Periclean perfection,
As though some ancient virtue,
Entered a larchwood country house,
Declaring:
> *In heaven I was reborn*
> *And the gate for me became a harp.*
> *The path a ribbon…*
> *The Host – I see through the grain,*
> *And already Emanuel lives on*
> *Mount Tabor again.*

    5.

And how Poland was present – in the notes – with
The absolute perfection of history,
In a rainbow of rapture, at her zenith –
Poland of the transformed legendary
Wheelwrights – the same
Of the Golden-Bee.
(I would recognize her at the farthest edge of being.)

6.

And behold – you song complete – and no longer
Can I see you – yet once more – I hear
Something?  Like a childish quarrel –
And still the clash of keys
Over the song's unsingable desire –
And nudging themselves out of silence –
In eights – in fives –
The strings murmur: *Has he begun to play?*
*Or does he spurn us again?*

7.

You!  Who are the profile of love,
Whose name is fulfillment,
That – which in Art is designated style,
What permeates and animates the shape of song and stone…
You – what history terms *Epoch*,
Where there is neither that, nor a golden age,
You will join together : the Spirit and the Letter,
And *Consummatum est…*
You – the consummate expression,
However yours – the Sign – and wherever,

Whether in Phidias?  In David?  Or in Chopin?
Or on the stage of Aeschylus?
Always a certain lack will take its revenge,
The stigma, that on this globe, there is want.
Fulfillment?  Only hurts it!
This – to awaken the urge,
The urge to continually cast in front of us…as payment.
A spike of wheat?  Ripened like a golden comet,
Barely stirred by a breeze,
That will shower forth seeds
Scattered by its very perfection.

8.

Look, Frederyk – behold – Warsaw,
Under the blazing star,
Strangely aglow –

Look – the organ at St. John's – your nest
And there – old patrician homes praised -
Old as the Polish Common-Wealth –
Cobblestone squares mute and gray,
In the clouds, King Zygmunt's sword is raised.

9.

Look! In alleys and backstreets –
Cossack horses darting around
Like swallows before a storm,
Shooting in the sky, ahead of the troops –
Hundreds of them – hundreds –
A building blazes – the flames die down –
Then flare up again – and there – at the wall –
The foreheads of mourning widows
The rifle butts strike…

And once more I see, though blinded by smoke –
Furniture – something coffin-like
That shows through the columns on a balcony,
They hoist it up…it crashes down…down…you Piano!

10.

That – which proclaimed in a hymn of ecstasy
Poland at its height –
The absolute perfection of History,
Poland of the transformed legendary Wheelwrights –
That very thing crashed on the cobblestone's granite.

Behold – how noble thought
Is trampled by human fury –

Just as – throughout all time –
Everything that will awaken they deny.
And behold – Orpheus' body
Mutilated by the Maenad's thousand passions,
While each one wails: *Not me,*
*Not me...* Teeth gnashing.

    11.

But you? But me? Let us strike up a song that atones:
*Rejoice – future grandson – in defeat...*
Thus uttered the mute cobblestones:

*The Ideal – came down – to the street.*

Postcard "Chopin evoquant ses souvenirs de Pologne" based on a painting by Jan Styka. Braun & Cie., Editeurs, Salon de Paris, ca. 1900. Maja Trochimczyk Collection.

# Chopin's Piano

## Charles Adés Fishman

> *On September 19, 1863, fourteen years
> after Chopin's death, Russian soldiers
> in Warsaw hurled his piano to the street
> from a fourth-floor window.*

We were not there to hear it
and all the witnesses are gone

but the sound of that falling lingers

They came at dawn to play it
and were deafened by the drone

We were not there to hear it

Not a chord could please the ear
each note jarred to the bone

We were not there to hear it

But such maestros tire soon:
they would write mazurkas   études

with bayonets and guns

We were not there to hear it
but we've learned the tune.

# Ruby and Sapphire

Kerri Buckley

Evening belongs to Chopin,
crimson silks and sparkling wines, trails of smoke

From balconies, stiff, rustling fabrics of
tailored suits, perfume, chocolate truffles rolled in

Waxed paper cones, shiny as diamonds, as pearls,
and the music — notes one breathes in, holds fully

So it might never
be forgotten, sound of richness, of ruby, of sapphire,

Elegant nod to all refined things,
to the ivory on a piano key, thrown from a window

Into a golden glitter of leaves by Russian soldiers

# The Enemy is in the House

Martin Willitts, Jr.

> "The enemy is in the house (...) Oh God, do you exist? You do and yet you do not avenge. - Have you not had enough of Moscow's crimes - or - or are You Yourself a Muscovite (...) I here, useless! And I here empty-handed. At times I can only groan, suffer, and pour out my despair at my piano!"
> — Chopin, 1831, learning that Poland had been defeated by Russian armies.

The piano cannot stop wars, nor lift the dead,
nor block the door. I am numb, empty handed,
wondering why you cannot stop this silence
deadly as bullets. There are no avenging angels crying.
The Russians are shooting notes of despair
and all I can do is huddle in the sheet music of snow.
Paris is the gathering place of defeated friends,
failed politicians, grieving mothers and wounded artists.
There are exiles everywhere speaking Polish sadness.
I cannot pound the keys on my piano loud enough.
I shall never return to my homeland.
I shall not give in to the Russian demands.
I shall not let one note from my fingers serve them.
The enemy is in the house.
It does not mean they can trample the rugs with mud.
We have a saying where I come from.
If a stranger stays uninvited, then call him a friend
and mistreat him like a friend, then he will go away
thinking your false friendship is real as butter on bread.
It is like playing with a piano one-handed. It can be done,
but not as well as with two hands.
It is like a gun without bullets.
It is like a person without a home.

Postcard "F. Chopin Music and Visions" with a fragment of the Nocturne in F-sharp Major, Op. 15, No. 2 and a vision of the Łazienki Palace in Warsaw. Published Nakładem Braci Rzepkowicz in Warsaw, Poland, c. 1900s-1910s. Maja Trochimczyk Collection.

# More Polish than Poland

Millicent Borges Accardi

Light-hands,
Embark
Then stop.

He dreams of
Where he died many
Times in a French
Novel.

Colors begin
Like a quickening.

Erotic transports,
Modulations,
Clouds taking on fantastic shapes.

Chopin is
playing Polish
Folk music.

The piano,
A solo instrument.

The child,
absorbed everything,
and the night is all up around us.

# G

Roxanne Hoffman

G,

*I tell my piano*
*the things I used to tell you,*
pull back its fallboard
after propping up the lid,
stroke its sturdy trusses,
hear the strings vibrate in sympathy,
undampered escapement permits,
as my fingers depress and release its keys
to unlock unsaid thoughts,
the music I dream.
The solid back frame
understands the balanced tension
of romance:
the give and the take
of the player and the played,
the rhythm of two heartbeats, even at rest,
the somber melody
of disharmony.
We of equal temperament
speak at length,
practice our arpeggios and scales,
regulate our voices,
and play Mozart in your absence.

F.

Note: Lines 1 and 2 are a quotation attributed to Chopin. Toward the end of his life he had a falling out with his long time love George Sand, they separated, and she was absent from his funeral. A final request of Chopin's was to have Mozart's *Requiem* sung in his memory. After his death, among his possessions, a lock of her hair was found in a small envelope embroidered with their initials "G.F" tucked in the back of his diary.

# I Tell My Piano the Things I Used to Tell You

Jessica Day

> "It is dreadful when something weighs on your mind, not to have a soul to unburden yourself to. You know what I mean. I tell my piano the things I used to tell you."
>
> Frédéric Chopin

You may cough, wander moors, perform,
laugh, write or weep. Everyone is
doing just that this October.
White, milky skies close overhead;
icy, metallic hills underfoot;
landscapes played in black keys.

Tear down the scale on a Pleyel,
take some visits while I wait for you.
Think awhile. *How alike: Scotland
and Poland. How to be sure when one
is actually dead? How women enter in flesh
and leave in song.* Then thunderstorms.

Tears seem strange, but necessary.
What a sad but blessed little thing:
to live awhile, to write awhile,
love awhile maybe. But that adagio
final movement – these are the things
I would talk about if you were here.

# Preludes

# A Minor Prelude

—after Chopin—

Leonard Kress

Two stories—and there it is, for all to hear,
a trill, propelled along the arc of a pointed toe,
limbering the rest, at rest between lesser
Polonaises. Ballet studio window propped open.
17th and Walnut. Early fall.

The way it always is when I walk by.
It trails me, swarms. Commingles with the subway pitch
squalling through underworlds.
And it's still there, rehearsing those first frank
few floating bars, tipsy and homeless.

Even as the subway creeps—up the trellis
over Fishtown and Harrowgate, and all my fellow
passengers secretly binge on the spectacle below,
forty steps or so, down from the El platform,
past the first few shot and beer bars.

But way back there, at the other
barre, the one who got me going,
no longer the cynosure of dried sweat
and slumped dancers peeling off layers—
the pianist knows this is not home,
out among cobbles, searching among ringing chords,
preparing to scale hidden alley walls.
When will his arch fingers reach their destination?
One hand does, the other soon evicts.
Mattress, chest, easy chair come crashing down

like Chopin's piano from the Cossacked Zamoyski Palace.
He thinks of Bach, who never ventured far,
reprising his return, welcome and expected.
Or is it Schubert, barely extricating all those keys,
warily glancing at, as he leaves, the lock?

Postcard "Frederic François Chopin," with an excerpt from
his Nocturne No. 2. Dates of life and death printed on the reverse.
New York: Music-Art Co. n.d., ca 1920. Maja Trochimczyk Collection.

## Prelude in Majorca

Christine Klocek-Lim

The wet day carried rain into night
as he composed alone.
With each note he wept
and music fell on the monastery,
each note a cry for breath
his lungs could barely hold.
Even as his world
dissolved around him
"into a terrible dejection,"
he played that old piano in Valldemosa
until tuberculosis didn't matter;
until the interminable night
became more than a rainstorm,
more than one man sitting alone
at a piano, waiting
"in a kind of quiet desperation"
for his lover to come home
from Palma.

When Aurore finally returned
"in absolute dark"
she said his "wonderful Prelude,"
resounded on the tiles of the Charterhouse
like "tears falling upon his heart."
Perhaps she is right.
Or perhaps Chopin "denied
having heard" the raindrops.
Perhaps in the alone
of that torrential night

he created his music simply
to hold himself inside life
for just one note longer.

Notes:

Prelude No.15 in D-flat Major, Op. 28.

Quotes from *Histoire de Ma Vie* (*History of My Life*, vol. 4) by George Sand (Aurore, Baronne Dudevant).

Postcard of Chopin and Sands's residence at Valldemossa, Mallorca, based on a painting by Erwin Hubert. Maja Trochimczyk Collection.

# Raindrop Prelude

### After Chopin's Prelude, in D-flat Major, Opus 28, No. 15

Richard Pflum

Raindrop repeating on my window sill,
hypnotically beating on my window sill:
Captive in my cell, I lean against the damp
clinging to granite walls, their chiseled bulk.
And I am a bird without a wing waiting
like a drop, then free falling, a beat
sustained by the pure water of the air,
an accompaniment for singing though
amplifying all that is still, here inside
a music never quite fading after its final cadence.

# Chopin's "Raindrop"

Cheryl M. Thatt

A steady rain
drop
drips down
insistent as the minutes
he looks out the window
cannot escape *it*.

He translates rain
drop
damp spirit
travels inward
passionate
notes whittle away the dreary
steady rain
drop
a clock
in the distance punctuates the gray day
wrestling with his own dark language
his soft fingers caress the keys to sanity
slowly he shapes adversary into ally…
pounds out melancholy
drop
by precious damn drop…

A steady rain
drop
dripped down
like the click of a shutter
slippery hours
captured forever.

# A Pastoral Piece in D-flat Major

Ben Humphrey

Gently beating on a window pane,
a rain storm's motif
usually a patter, *pianissimo*,
like repetitious figures of a Chopin prelude.

There are grace notes in raindrops,
a passing pastoral theme and a final
closed cadence. An atmospheric disturbance
has occupied center stage.

*Largo*, after Prelude in E minor, Op. 28, No. 4,
Plate III in *Three Preludes of Chopin Interpreted by Sigismond Ivanowski*.
Drawn by Ivanovski, half-tone plates engraved by H. Davidson.
New York: F. C. Gordon, n.d.  Maja Trochimczyk Collection.

# Prelude in D-Flat Major, Opus 28, No. 15

Carrie A. Purcell

You have to
my teacher said
think of that note like rain,
steady, but who,
my teacher said
wants to hear only that?

On Majorca in a monastery
incessant coughing
covered by incessant composition
and everywhere dripping

*sotto voce*
move the rain lower
let it fill the space left in your lungs
let it triumph

We die so often
we don't call it dying anymore

# Minor Detour Through an Old Neighborhood

Marianne Worthington

The apartment complex
at Arbor Place where I shared

a one-bedroom with my cousin
bears the derelict face of abuse.

Doors and windows missing
or kicked in reveal the shadowed

faces of a few squatters, their wary
eyes are abandoned rooms.

The fear of ruin stings
my throat. What happened

to my old neighborhood where half
a block away the bungalows root

in the manicured lawns like oaks
and in one of those houses

I studied piano with a gentle
man who stood behind me

and pushed my shoulders down
and said *breathe here* and

*pianissimo* and *rubato, rubato,*
as I played the "Raindrop Prelude"?

# After Listening to All the Preludes

Nils Peterson

End of day. Almost autumn. We stand
between a red sun sliding behind the distant hills
and a gray-silver moon rising into a field of gray-blue
still caught in the miracle of the Preludes,
all of them, one after the other, a sea of notes,
sometimes calm, sometimes storm,
an ocean of beginnings, like life,
each day, each hour, each minute
a prelude, and our continuous wondering – to what?

Now, after this prelude, a soft September evening.

# Etudes

# Etude

Elisabeth Murawski

as a boy he slept
with bits of wood
between his fingers

to increase their span
now he plays
to breathe   to last

past this country house
under the chestnuts
taming the keys

of Madame Skarbek's piano
pouring notes
against the night

that is falling
eyes destined to close
on a ceiling not in Poland

whose soul in his hands
will flower
circumnavigate the globe

# Chopin Etude

Joseph Somoza

On this quiet night
that will not return to speak again
ever, though I shall invite it.

On this mild, early summer evening
with the breeze blowing from Chihuahua

that along the way has rattled tiles
on an adobe roof
and made an old man catch his breath,

I sit with the window open
and listen to the breeze Chopin heard
one hundred fifty years ago

the same waves
curling into themselves and back
the same gusts rushing at the dark.

# There Is No Other Love

### After Chopin's Etude in E Major, Opus 10, No. 3

R. Romea Luminarias

*—for Annie*

November sunlight peers
Between leaf-veins. Oval windows.
Rose petals on velvet. Autumn vines our arms
Glazed with ripeness, steeped in unrestrained embrace.
Tongues stilled; drought-pained mouths this one now-love alone

Can heal. Our Love steers
Unknown universes' oceans of shadows,
Maps red coral galaxies. Anemone-meteors swarm
Around us, stir hunger's hull knifing waves, probing abysses.
There is no other love obtains the soul, breaks open steel and stone;

There is no other Love destroys this present, ancient drought, this fall
Stripped bare of songs, deprived of harvest; there is no other Love sees
Through storms of swirling fires; only this love, O this our Love alone:
No other Love ordains, builds up the spirit, breathes life into dry bones.

# A Study with Cherries

Maja Trochimczyk

*After Etude in C Major, Op. 10, No. 1 and the cherry orchard
of my grandparents, Stanisław and Marianna Wajszczuk*

I want a cherry,
a rich, sweet cherry
to sprinkle its dark notes
on my skin, like rainy preludes
drizzling through the air.

Followed by the echoes
of the piano, I climb
a cherry tree to find rest
between fragile branches
and relish the red perfection –
morning cherry music.

Satiated, sleepy,
I hide in the dusty attic.
I crack open the shell
of a walnut to peel
the bitter skin off,
revealing white flesh –
a study in C Major.

Tasted in reverie,
the harmonies seep
through light-filled cracks
between weathered beams
in Grandma's daily ritual
of Chopin at noon.

Postcard of a young Chopin. Dresden: Max Sinz, No. 6 in Author and Composer Series. New York: Excelsior Post Card Co., ca. 1900-1910. Maja Trochimczyk Collection.

*from* Part First————————Chopin's Feet

Mark Tardi

> I much prefer the Chopin that reaches me in the street
> from an open window to the Chopin served in great style
> from the concert stage.
>
> <div align="right">Witold Gombrowicz, <i>Diary</i></div>

Surround tables.
Severaled.
That still.
Slight graces shown
without.

On your other neck
A more complex
permission.

Midnight or next.

On every other stairway
negative sets.

A long ago if.
If you choose.

If slowly.

All the more so as showers.

Only begun unburned

A composition of pillars
A fallcoat
A longing for other cities


We met less and less often

As finger or floorboard

spitting basins full
quivering
or else with effort


One night to fold out


An arch-delicate
A perhaps table


Red clefts

Those palpable facts which

Never made of so many

Both arrived today
while staying at

no. 7 in C-sharp minor

Our    scented water
        disconsolate


falling on the curtains

What might be carried in a jar

lain on top of light

    a brilliant
as to inscribe regret

I bowed, turned

Yet ourselves at each moment

      his catalogue
a forensic eloquence

It's very close now
unhurried

These tasks
         only cut shadows

Several keys so that

|  |  |
|---|---|
| | to variances |
| How he took the repeat | table into scales |
| the palaced while | that place of ragged |
| | correspondence |
| as if a chair<br>buried by lips | down worked |
| | Or take something for your |
| irresolutions | |
| | just as night exhausts itself |
| | at shoulder knots |
| | at all elaborate |

It was the silence that kept.
The vanish of the simplest givens.

Well-tailored.
Left between.
Bright fingers dangling.
The only informal you.

# Mazurkas

# Mazurka, Formed of Rain

Kathi Stafford

> "If he (Chopin) had not had the misfortune of meeting George Sand, who poisoned his whole being, he would have lived to be Cherubini's age."
> —Count Grzymała

Perhaps he missed
forty-two years of life
thanks to Sand. Her real
name: Aurore.

Maybe she ruined him,
killed him at age thirty-nine,
or blessed him.
Maybe twenty
mazurkas were lost
in the missed decades.

Turn the music into verse
then list the notes in squares.

Build the etude room
by room. Plaster up the walls,
the phrase of cool grace.

Would he say, *It was worth it,*
*she brought notes*
*as gifts, coins*
*in my purse—*

speed and volume
so indefinite

but starting
movements that build
up the revolution
and menace.

Look at notes,
read the measures—

feel the fight
they lived so that he could spin this song

Austrian postcard based on a painting by Leo B. Eichhorn,
Published by BKWI (Bruder Kohn) in Vienna, ca. 1900s-1910s.
Maja Trochimczyk Collection.

# Sewing with Chopin

Katrin Talbot

As needle and thread
quieted the hem,
Mazurkas
too sad to dance to
serenaded my stitching

and the aching sadness
urged me to keep sewing
all through the day,

mending moments of
heartbreak, hope deferred,
misty loss

while I sat across from Chopin
and listened attentively
as he spoke so eloquently
of the advantages of

a delicate
life

# Harvesting Chopin

## Maja Trochimczyk

> *After Mazurka in F-sharp Minor, Op. 59, No. 3, for my Grandma Nina, Uncle Galakcyon, and Father, Aleksy Trochimczyk*

The straw was too prickly,
the sunlight too bright,
my small hands too sweaty
to hold the wooden rake
my uncle carved for me.
I cried on the field of stubble;
stems fell under his scythe.

I was four and had to work –
Grandma said – no work no food.
How cruel! I longed for
the noon's short shadows
when I'd quench my thirst
with cold water, taste
the freshly-baked rye bread

sweetened by the strands
of music wafting from
the kitchen window.
Distant scent of mazurkas
floated above the harvesters
dressed in white, long-sleeved shirts
to honor the bread in the making

The dance of homecoming
and sorrow – that's what
Chopin was in the golden air
above the fields of Bielewicze
where children had to earn their right
to rest in the daily dose of the piano –
too pretty, too prickly, too bright

## Mazurka vs. the Day

Katrin Talbot

There are mornings,
Autumn Mornings so brilliant
so articulated
so crisp
When a Chopin Mazurka
silently collides with
the Day spirit

A day so radiant and joyful that
a melancholy dance can
only tug at the beauty

yearning for a joining,
a fusion of unmeasurable
sadness
with dazzling spirit

and the Day
Resists

# How to Make a Mazurka

Maja Trochimczyk

> *After Mazurka in A Minor, Op. 17, No. 4,*
> *for my Grandparents, Stanisław and Marianna Wajszczuk,*
> *who could play and bake their mazurkas like no one else*

Take one cup of longing
for the distant home that never was,
one cup of happiness that danced
with your shadows on the walls

of Grandpa's house, while he played
a rainbow of folk tunes
on his fiddle, still adorned
with last wedding's ribbons

      mix it – round and round to dizziness

stir in some golden buzz of the bees
in old linden tree, add the ascent
of skylark above spring rye fields,
singing praises to the vastness of blue

      mix it – round and round to dizziness

add chopped walnuts, figs, dates
and raisins, pour in some juice
from bittersweet grapefruit
freshly picked in your garden

      mix it – round and round to dizziness

add dark grey of rainclouds in Paris
that took Chopin back to the glimmer
of candles in an old cemetery
on the evening of All Souls' Day

      mix it – round and round to dizziness

bake it in the cloudless heat
of your exile, do not forget to sprinkle
with a dollop of sparkling crystals,
first winter's snowflakes at midnight

# Polonaises

# Polonaise

### Elisabeth Murawski

In the museum, along
with first editions,
the death mask, the chair

whose arms he gripped
in coughing fits,
a lock of yellow hair.

Was it Sand who clipped it
for a keepsake? She
who whispered

*Let me be your lightning rod*
as Chopin played
for her ears only,

courting the angels,
stealing the shine
from the Seine. Think

of his wish (a drastic
death certificate)
to have his body opened

*that I not be buried alive,*
of his heart taken home
to a Warsaw church,

of the grave in Père Lachaise
brilliant with roses
and candles, baskets

laden with fruit, of notes
plucked from his roots
that go on singing.

# A Good Death

John Z. Guzlowski

My father says
in time he'll learn
to listen to the Polonaise
and not hear Sikorski
or Warsaw, the hollow surge
and dust of German tanks,

only Chopin,
his staff of clean notes
and precise legato.

His dreams will be
of crystalled trees,
papered gifts
in red half-light,
the smell of warm sheds
and girls drawing milk
from waiting cows.

The snow will fall
and go unnoticed.

Austrian postcard with a portrait of Chopin by Eichert.
Vienna: BKWI (Bruder Kohn), c. 1900-1910. The series
also includes a portrait of pianist Ignacy Jan Paderewski.
Maja Trochimczyk Collection

# Polonaise for Justyna

Gabriel Shanks

Temerity squalls in tight circles
under your right hand,
the hand of six years old,
the hand mother didn't teach.
G Minor. Basic, brutal, flat.

Can you win her in the bridge, I wonder?
The innocence forced, even here,
Where she looks on and marvels.

But whirlpools return, shards of want,
impressing and stunned,
solemn and semiquaver,
tiny space between tones,
it hangs there, mothers, sons.

# How I Fell in Love with Chopin

Kath Abela Wilson


he did not own a piano
hesitant shy unsure

I brought him to my mother's house
where the old upright
moved in by seminarians last winter
still leaked snow

frail on the long walk
uphill he carried
the polonaises

told me how
he'd had polio as a child
came breathless to the bench
transfixed

we were all long afternoon
turned to dark
white moon balanced
ebony benched the sky

polished sound and circumstance
power I leaned into

he moved into my small apartment
took my mother's piano apart to rework it
keys scattered everywhere
for three years

it did not last

I had to collect them in a box

I don't think it ever got back together
but I realized in that time

I had fallen in love
with Chopin

# Waltzes

# Waltz

Lori Desrosiers

A bright night in Paris,
The ladies galore in their hats and bright frocks,
twirl—hems sweeping the floor.

Fredéric Chopin is cutting the rug
with Georges Sand, the writer;
her real name Aurore.

Ah, to touch while they danced,
what a daring display, such a joy –
some say waltzing will lead you astray.

So, dance with her, Chopin,
forget your consumption.
Put your piano-worn hands

to her corseted waist,
and one, two, three
one, two, three, dance.

# This Waltz is not For Dancing

### Chopin's Waltz in A Minor (Posthumous)

Lois P. Jones

Melody circles like a falcon in your parlor,
as if a note were a bird charmer who knows
my thoughts by name. I draw close
to your shadow, peeling like a corner of this dove-

colored wallpaper, a flammable bird you ignite.
It's not for me to hold onto souvenirs,
glittered towers bought for cheap
on the chalk-marked streets. Kiosks

with mildewed books sold for a few francs.
Nothing to rustle in the palm
but a mother-of-pearl-button on my blouse. So far
now from the sour smell of cesspools—

the horse-drawn barrels that carry things away
in the night. My silence urges you on,
pushes toward your colors
a form that will not stay fixed,

but shapes into twilight. Its deep blue reaches in
moist and transparent in your hands. I release
what storms I've gathered—my travels through them,
the journey of stairs climbed to catch the drop

of a single note. And you, oblivious of the rain
in your fingers, the gilt of dusk on the rue,
silky as a Mirabelle plum. Unconscious of my dream
of summer, a country dance and this song born of roses.

# Waltz in A Minor

Russell Salamon

*for Frédéric Chopin*

Women detach from birch trees
and come to lose themselves
under his fingers in music, while
rain falls on autumn streets. He
caresses perfect little infinities
into their sighs. Drops of sweat
slide between their breasts.

He plays a woman as if she were
a nocturne; her thighs moistening
with music. She hears herself
dissolve in perfect Eden—fresh soul
made from tones in A Minor and light.

For the woman who said No
he makes future lovers, music
for open eyes, waltz audiences
from deep centuries listening
to his hands say what women
know is true, and what they
weep for.

# Gdańsk

Dean Pasch

An old man recounts
The cracks in the pavement youth
He never lived through
Yet never left

A tug boat pulls out memories
Of Gdańsk's palimpsest harbour
And across choppy waves
In his faltering thoughts
Chopin's Waltz in A Minor
Dances with seagulls

Wings displace wind
Sunlight sneaks through
Cover of cloud
Catching the eye

Of one seagull's intent on more
On more than feathers
Or departure or arrival

His mother once told him
Without dreams his soup
Would taste bitter
Without love his life
Would too

The old man retires to bed
With his tugboat and a glint
In his eyes
For his beloved Gdańsk
And the waltz of a youth
That haunts him
Even now

# An Invitation in D-flat Major

Ben Humphrey

Snowfall over, sun's out,
wind whistles a Waltz,
refracting flakes whirl in triple time.

My focus limited
to page, paragraph.
Sun warms my cabin's roof.

A crescendo of clattering slabs
awakens me from my book
calls me – to take a Minute for the dance.

# Minute Waltz

Marlene Hitt

Black keys, three and two,
among white ranks
strode beneath my Auntie's hands.
I was warm as I sat beside her.
Music hovered like crystals around moons
as Auntie's hands threw flakes of Chopin
to drift down to my hair.
My eager hand poised, untrained, pale
over strings, then keys, ready
while time took the music for its own.
Through her hands flowed Auntie's
dwindling moments, her breath
coming harsh and labored, her arms
reaching for the highest notes
to make beautiful even the air
around the sickness in her lungs
and her dying, and the last sounds
of the Minute Waltz.

Postcard *The Last Chords of Chopin*, based on a painting
by Fr. Klimes, *Les derniers accords de Chopin*. Published by BKWI
(Bruder Kohn) in Vienna, Austria, c. 1900-1910.
Maja Trochimczyk Collection.

# My One-Minute Waltz

## Taoli-Ambika Talwar

Grass
kissed
running
bride's
feet

wind
blew
in to
center
of
spaces

his
fingers
ran across
the keys
mind
lessly

birds
loudly
sang
amid
trees

sun
came
went
trickling

through
leaves
my
heart
raced
to
drums
on mountain
tops

all life
chose
to live
happy

free
surren
der

mothers
lovers
muses

ate *pâté*
on crack
ers
wine

bubbled
in plenty

so
world
came
to
be still.

And
babies
were born
crying
into
our
hearts

eating
of nip
ples hold
ing
eyes to
eyes
such
bewilder
ment
then
love

home
to
stay

learn
laws
of
earth
life
pain

to
joy
ordeals

chances
we
practice
to
choose

the love
that
abides
with self

that is
made
with
music

A life
waltzes
to
unique
dreams

passions
of all
lands

center
in us

my tears
fill
your

cups
yours
my palms

we're
drenched

light

Now
I am
alive
in you

because
of you

Music
jumps
out of

scatters
in the
world
from
our
hands.

# Chopin's Minute Waltz

### Clark Crouch, Cowboy Poet

Chopin was popular
as folks moved to the west,
from salons to saloons,
he was among the best.

Dancing the Minute Waltz,
two-stepping to that tune,
the way that cowboys do,
they thought it'd end too soon.

Hats, rakish on their heads,
their worn boots shining bright,
dancing the night away,
it was a won'drous sight.

They pranced with much ado,
bowing and gyrating
with ladies, oh so fair,
desire unabating.

Someone said 'twas classic,
not a tune for dance halls,
and cowboys took offense,
got ready for some brawls.

Chopin would have been proud
as they stood up for him
and took claim to that waltz,
their faces looking grim.

Chopin sure was noted
for other tunes as well,
but on that waltz at least
they'd follow him to hell.

# Chopin: Thoughts a-Waltz

Sharon Chmielarz

Slow dance. And dramatic.
His moves, fast.
I like a fast man.
He has found there are more
exciting things to do than eat.

Walking he notices every riff
over the pond's surface.
Summer. All a body can do.

Work circles the city where he lives.
The peasants', the miller's, the mother's, the sawyer's.
Work drives deeper into the city where the beggar
sits at the gate. Listen to the composer,
making up life.

A quiet boy has his place
elaborated in a constellation.
Companions on their way,
a competition within the hand.

Down among the bullrushes, a cold fish
who cares for nothing like love.

Providence, waiting.
We slip through a crack
safely.

A blue dog rollicks. A log stuck crosswise
plays itself out. O, sweet rocketing.

The skirt waltzes, flashing, just enough
wine in the wearer's brain to be giddy.

# Waltzing with Chopin in a Foreign Land

Taoli-Ambika Talwar

*for Maja Trochimczyk*

She smiles she smiles
she carefree smiles
remembering her dancing
to Chopin in the garden:

sometimes the garden
was dressed in white
specially when little meadow flowers
pushed through to meet sky

and music of pattering feet
met squealing delight
of children hungrily
watching warm cakes

fresh out of the oven
and picklesoup waiting
for eager mouths
rosepetal jam that *jaju* loved

Teatime with Chopin
whose feet moved through across
the floors at home
waiting for warmth

through rough times
called winter: she smiles
sometimes sad and wistful
for here the tea tastes not same

But she can dress in white
to remember the land that was all white
naked and marked with pianos
whose rugged fingers
would still play to bring
angels down to earth

for when the angels came
she felt she'd be safe even tho'
she didn't always believe it:

But somehow there are always roses
in her landscape, even jam—
that is how she practiced the waltz
and never forgot—

As the old hearth faced north
her heart had to grow big
to contain her story and her smile
that shines in white: glows

like her eyes warm soft moist
as her poems…Chopin falls
like rain sometimes…

# 19 Chopin Waltzes

Emily Fragos

Snow falls from rafters of pink, swollen clouds;
moonlight drenches the peasants' fields.
The feathered flesh of a fish, the juice of a peach,
the silver rivers before we named them with color.
All the begetting: the weak limbs and soft bellies,
the faces elongated like the devil himself. The devil
himself! The ship that sails through dreams of Achilles.
The palace of the deaf. The murmuring in centuries' rooms,
the crying of turtle doves, the fleet-footed dancing.
On Earth as in heaven, beauty without reason.

# Nocturnes

# Nocturne: Chopin in Vienna

Elisabeth Murawski

Drawn to the cathedral's
darkest corner, its *mournful
harmony* of stone, young Chopin

stands beside a Gothic pillar,
tombs behind him and beneath.
*I'm only lacking one above.* Soon

the nave will blaze with lights
for midnight Mass, the first
worshipers drift in. Their joy

will only fuel his melancholy.
Turning up the collar of his cloak,
he steals from the cathedral

for music at the palace. To be
distracted. To stop hearing
in his head *sierota*, the Polish word

for orphan. Afterwards, he paces
in his room without a view.
*I've never felt so clearly*

*my loneliness.* What to do?
Stay here in Vienna? Paris
tempts him. Warsaw's home. Broods

in his dressing gown. Yesterday
he stumbled on the funeral
of a stranger, coffin bobbing

through a crowd of mourners.
He tried not to stare
at their faces slack with grief.

The gleam of the highly polished
wood courted his eyes
like an impossible lover.

E. Цичкиевичъ, Ноктюрнъ Шопэна. *(E. Cickiewicz, Chopin's Nocturne).*
Postcard published in Russia, ca. 1900. Maja Trochimczyk Collection.

# Mazovian Willows

### Chopin's Nocturne, Opus 9

Linda Nemec Foster

> *What has happened to my heart? I can*
> *hardly remember how they sing at home.*
> *~ Chopin*

Did the strain of a mazurka
split you in two? Don't
tell me lightning, wind,
harsh betrayal of nature —
anything that has logic.
As much logic as a Polish
composer with a French name
who wrote scores of music
for a single instrument;
who was in love with a strong
woman who adopted a man's
name because she liked
simplicity. No logic there,
old tree, stark willow.
You probably gave Frédéric
his inspiration: one
note at a time drowning out
the sky, changing your life
from a single vision
to a double one. A split
trunk resembling a pair
of hands in prayer, bruised
fingers of the émigré. Your
country not even listed
on the map. Perhaps it wasn't

a mazurka that cut your
heart in two: one side
listing to the West, the other
firmly planted in Mazovia,
despite itself.
Perhaps it was a simple
nocturne, the last fading
light before night comes
and eyes close. Music
of good-bye, farewell;
the knowledge of never
going home again. Music
of exile that almost forgets
the language of the earth.

# Chopin's Sonnet

Nocturne in D-flat Major, Op. 27, No. 2

David Ellis

In 1834 Chopin composed
a sonnet—a lyric unconstrained
by quatrains, couplets, or pentameters.

A night piece, rhymes and meters scripted
in the air, crafted in silences of evening
slowly, *Lento sostenuto*, as stars move

dolce with ornamental notes and trills,
appoggiaturas sung in one breath,
*cantabile*, to tune the evening air.

In 2004 Maestro Leon Fleisher
sentenced to thirty five years
of silence by focal hand Dystonia,

released himself and, unconstrained,
splashed the D-flat Major Nocturne
with soft measures of moonlight,

*Lento sostenuto*, in a nightscape
of *bel canto*, an Evensong
for Chopin's perfect poem.

# The Last Nocturne

Jarek Gajewski

He does not look out anymore
from his apartment window
in the courtyard on the 1st floor
at 12 Place Vendôme

Nor whispers to Ludwika
simple Polish words
cutting air wings of white doves
their alike profiles facing each other
tied up in taciturn love

Past midnight
a clock strikes twice
October's day of 17th
sleeps still in darkness
The last nocturne of moribundity
has been started without faux pas
It is time for mourning arrival
and quiet departure of his life
in the year 1849

# Waiting For Fingers, For Keys

Jennifer S. Flescher

Her doorway, breasts
and baby-grand

*waiting for*
fingers, for keys.

Chopin is dead.
*Still, Nocturne*

plays. Ice curtains
brace the window –

Glaze, a drift, her whole
house, suddenly

transitory, see-through
passages – passed

ages, movements,
water-time concertos.

Through the ceiling,
the casements,

years – passed
yesterday's firm frame.

# Nocturne No. 6 in G Minor

## Rosemary O'Hara

*For where your treasure is, there will your heart be also.*

1.
On a misty autumn morning in Seattle,
a woman opens her piano,
enters Chopin's melancholy world.
Makes acquaintance with melodic dissonance,
becomes intimate with his chromaticism.

2.
A plaintive melody rises and sighs,
a clock-like bass marks time.
Volume waxes and wanes,
*fortissimo, pianissimo.*
Accented chords clash
louder, faster –
*crescendo, accelerando;*
slower, softer –
*ritardando, diminuendo.*

After three bass notes,
like tolling of a bell,
treble and bass join
in *religioso.*
Hymnlike chords divide –
attack, detach,
*sforzato, staccato.*
Fading to pianissimo,
six sustained chromatic chords.

3.
Chopin penned nocturnes
in the alpha and omega of his life,
his first at 17, his last at 36.
At 23, he captures
his first love's voice,
leaves Warsaw for Paris.

At 39, his blazing candle
wavers, fades. As he wished,
his heart sent back to Warsaw,
his body buried in Paris
between Bellini and Cherubini
in Père Lachaise.

Friends scatter
Polish soil
on his grave.

# Night Nocturne

Lucy Anderton

Played in the firelight,
the night holding up the house

in its remote glove, each tone
held in the dark

of my mouth—even Chopin
cannot return you.

This cold is so still
that each winter note is a call

out to any heart—but
yours will not visit. Not

pulled by even the hook of
this bruised nocturne. Won't you

answer, if only by note? Wrap it about
a sparrow's leg. Do you still dream

in glass? Does rain still look like Chopin
to you? With the night so busy

sewing liquid in my hair—
With the trees holding

their breath to watch
the scent of starlight slide

its easy tongue up
my back, tell me—Why

can't you be the Moon?
These notes? The things

that cover me in this simple way?
I tell you: in this jawbone of landscape

between us there are whole lives—
and dying, too—people spitting

blood out of cars—
and loving so hard

their hips bust. You
were never meant to stay.

I call out to you through these
phrases that ache, that suffer, so politely—

I call through the night
to the warm lantern of your heart.

# The Scarlet Hour

Kerri Buckley

—Chopin plays.

In red, beaded dress I
wander beaches of garnet sands

Beneath a golden sunset-drizzled
sky of painted scarlet watercolor streaks.

Holding red shoes and
Cabernet, pulling swirls of skirt to my knees

Bare feet crushing ruby grapes into rich
blood of the vine — it becomes my blood

*If you were here I'd explore the
softness of your mouth, ravage its*

*Sweetness like a gypsy pirate alone
with her captive, your absence a sharp*

*Thorn piercing your tender mouth where
keening rivers run crimson*

Restless seas scanned for sails on the horizon,
stretch of rubato in the Nocturnes arcs

Above the crashing surf and rushing spray.
Gulls grieve with me, overhead cries spiraling.

*We wait, the foamy sea and I, for your return*

# During Nocturne

### Nocturne No. 19 (in E Minor, Op. 72, No. 1)

Lia Brooks

First I am without ears
in the room of my mother.

Vibration from the valve open,
closing, is a rhythm iambic
here in the half-light.

Your music without sound,
my non-language poem hammers

cloth-covered on the strings
rolls through cloud—red
into the darkening through my limbs.

\*

It is only when my mother's pulse insists *This
is evening* and lays hands on the keys, that I find you
in my abdomen—the tremor of fingers, my new throat,

antiphonal here in water, night on it like reflections
of space. It expands outward in waves, measured
like tide, new moons, measured like the years in wood.

You do not ask if I am listening—it is already part
of the walls, nocturne of my sleep, river-sea psalm
which my mother explains with every bar, every note

you lifted from midnight's lip and made score. You call
for translation—the shift between white and black,
the sound and silences. And afterwards, I tell you this room

has fallen between daylight, remains so, out of days
and into seasons. That I am caught now
in these helter-skelter rings tree-bound to earth by circles.

*Nocturn.* Postcard with a painting by Br. Rychter Janowska,
from the cycle "W Starym Dworku"(In an Old Manor). Kraków:
Wydawnictwo Salonu Malarzy Polskich. Maja Trochimczyk Collection.

# Nocturnes in Spring

Leonore Wilson

In spring you played nocturnes,
Morning glories burst upon the vine.
There was always a certain melancholy
About you, Mother, the way you combed your hair,
Dark and wet back upon your face,
Pulling out the grey strands
One by one, gently letting them go
In the breeze, watching the wild canaries
Scatter after they divvied them up.
You noticed the cold air
In the morning tulips, the dew
On the oleander and wild rose,
The smell of jasmine and mint,
The budding sound of a chrysalis.
In playing nocturnes, you gathered
The smallest things. You taught me
To hear the rain feeding leaves,
The dance of a hummingbird's wings,
The difference between a pigeon
And a dove, their cooing
Not singing. A cloud's formation
Changing, a quail's echo
Rising and falling:
The want, the need,
The gentle music of your love.

# Chopin's Nocturnes Askew

Marie Lecrivain

I. (Nocturne in E-flat Major, Op. 9, No. 2)

I will not wax pastoral
in the twilight. At first,
reluctant to be drawn
into this realm of beauty,
I shift into wakefulness
at the full symphony
of crows cawing
harsh lullabies &
warm autumn breezes
blowing around us.
I know this interlude
is supposed to be
dramatic & fun,
but I am driven
to my knees,
trying desperately
not to weep
in the light
of your hope...
Why couldn't you
leave me alone?

## II. (Nocturne in E Major, Op. 62, No. 2)

Ahhh.... I've been
such a fool. As the
midnight hour
approaches,
you tease me
over my reluctance
to partake of this
amorous adventure.
Drowsy & flushed,
we lay nestled
among the roots
of the Tree of Life,
caressing each other's
limbs, wishing
to prolong the slow
ascendancy, the increased
play of passionate notes
swimming in our blood;
fuel to launch us
into the highest
reaches of Nothing,
until that moment,
– sated & timeless –
we fall back into
ourselves.

## III. (Nocturne in C-sharp Minor, Op. 27, No. 1)

Why are we trapped
in layers of familiarity
& contempt?
I suppose, in
these final hours,
anathema & ennui
are natural end-products
of a life lived
inside a nocturne
with you... &
it pains me
to see you flinch,
your smile shattering
at my touch.
I want to resist
the darkening
of memory, the
evaporation
of your kisses
grown dry...
at best, I hope
we will fade
into a faint melody
for future lovers
whose open ears &
upturned palms
will catch a soft
note or two
of what we
once were,
& what
again,
we will
be...

# Nocturne

> – after Chopin

Lola Haskins

i

Drawing the oval across measure
lines, he thinks: This Woman,
and combs with his fingers
her dark hair.
The scent of
jasmine lingers on his hands.

ii

A warm wind splits the song
into two streams of birds,
each yearning south.
He
lifts his pen, wanting to
stay their wings
high above
the flowered islands.

iii

Somewhere he has left Helena,
trailing her fingers
in the water.
He turns the pages.
The moon silvers the paper
where the notes sail,
the small dark
notes with their flags,
the whole notes with none.

# Chopin Nocturne

Victor Contoski

An old man leans against a piano
reaches his hands down to the keys
and plays a Chopin nocturne.
His wife
        a Hindu woman
dances slowly sensuously
        to the music
                without moving her body
                without moving her feet.
The notes pour over you
        like water.

# Eternal Nocturne

## Russell Salamon

*For Frédéric Chopin*

He sees the eternal nocturne.
All day he has been feeling
the cool of it in willow trees
on the road past golden
wheat fields. Now at the piano
light scuttles under his fingers.

He wants tones that leak life—
harvested wheat, fresh bread,
to the woman who said no. And
black butterflies whose shadowy
rhythms weep for a form that finds
fragments of perfect being—night
music where lost lovers find light.

# Sonatas and Other Works

# Tryst

### Chopin's Sonata for Cello and Piano, Op. 65

### Jean L. Kreiling

We think of him as one inclined to brood
alone, communing only with the keys
of his piano, dredging solitude
and self for deeply felt soliloquies.
But here he lets the hammered strings seduce
a stranger—one more sparsely strung, and bowed—
composing intimacies that unloose
impassioned dialogues. The minor mode
foreshadows troubled romance as they meet,
*Allegro moderato*; then they flirt
in *Scherzo* vacillations, wild and sweet,
until a plaintive *Lento* hints of hurt.
The last *Allegro* finds their tempers quick—
but lust has made their voices warm and thick.

# Thunder of Sorrow

### After Chopin's Piano Sonata in B-flat Minor, Opus 35, Third Movement: The Funeral March

Shayla Hawkins

Chopin's fingers
on piano keys
somber tone and tread

a thunder of aching and sorrow
as the soul enters the realm of the dead

Chopin's sonata
a drumming of death
pierced with whispers of light

like the sun's yellow fire rays
surrendered to the shroud
of the cooling indigo night

Relentless rhythm and warning
of the final fate of man

Chopin's fingers
on the piano
strong as a gravedigger's hands

*Chopin's Funeral March from Piano Sonata, Op. 35.*
Postcard published in Warsaw: Nakładem Braci Rzepkowicz, n.d.
Mailed in February 1911. Maja Trochimczyk Collection.

# Berceuse, Opus 57, in D-Flat

Meg Withers

A variety of feathered fans waft,
      as doorways empty of daughters.
           Dowagers scour the dance floor, and
    stovepipe men
breathe a blue haze in billiard rooms
          smoking cigars.
  Sweeping tulle veils
    shroud pale shoulders
          the pearl nape of neck,
     a sheer glimpse of ankle – everything
          emptying
   into light.

# Listening to Chopin's Ballades

Gretchen Fletcher

1839

Lit by candles
flickering on wall sconces
reflected in mirrors
dripping wax onto table tops
and even his precious Pleyel piano,
a small circle of friends and patrons
sits in his Paris apartment.
Women settle into semi-circled chairs
with a rustle of *peau de sois* skirts.
Candle flames send sparks
from jewels circling necks and wrists
and dangling from eager ears.
In a corner Sand sits in a halo of smoke,
comfortably-trousered legs crossed.
His hands hover over the keys.
No one dares cough.
His friends exhale only after he strikes
the opening two-octave C's in F major.

1959

Lit by the greenish glow from the stereo dial,
we lie on the floor of your apartment,
watching the record circle the turntable,
listening to the tweeter and woofer balancing
the sound of your prized LP –
Horowitz playing the Ballades.
Your arm pillows my head.

The album cover quotes Niecks:
"a quiver of excitement runs through"
the third and "the main theme...
recaptures happiness...every time it reappears."

    2009

The dimly lit memory reappears.
I see us, I hear the Chopin,
and I quiver with happiness.

*Molto Allegro*, after Prelude in C-sharp Minor, Op. 28, No. 10, Plate I in *Three Preludes of Chopin Interpreted by Sigismond Ivanovski*. Drawn by Ivanovski, half-tone plates engraved by H. Davidson. New York: F. C. Gordon, n.d. Maja Trochimczyk Collection.

# A Cry in the Woods

### Suggested by Chopin's Fantasy Impromptu in C-sharp Minor

Richard Pflum

Night winds from the northwest buffet living branches
fill dark voids between with turbulence, excesses of
howling air, crackles of light flashing sporadically
through a thicket on the horizon. It is only as night
calms, fades, and black is finally replaced by
a subtle but definite blue, when another sound
is heard from the recovering pines:

a hushed sound which finds solace as a human voice,
first questioning then accepting, still desperate in its choice
when finding the same grief repeated, then finally lost
at last, inside this glittering morning's white rush.

# Concerto No. 1, in E minor on Highway 111, Palm Springs

Ruth Nolan

Lifted, by the sudden desert wind
   just east of Palm Springs
      rounding Windy Point, 2 a.m.
could sprinkle those stars the way
your hands caress the keyboard
of your mother's piano until the lid slams
shut and father's voice commands you
to stop the noise, stop the noise

Caressed, by the windy desert mid-night,
   tickling your hair as you lean
      your head against the open window
tantalizes your imagination, you are 12 again
and your hands, together, devour the major
and minor keys until you are one
with the dark void, foot pressing down,
long chords that will linger into dawn

Hugged with warmth, this rushing air
   blowing ghosted windmill blades
      a 13,000 foot mountain in your eyes
voicing the crisp leaps up and down dorm
stairs with your first boyfriend, who taught
you that this was the musical master, after
all, and it all rushes back to you, this

Styled by elegance of motion, *staccato, fortissimo*
   cresting on the car stereo as you leapfrog
      between the lines on the highway
between the spaces of darkness and sound,
blown across the sand dunes into magnificence

# Life

# Night-Blooming Jasmine

Leonore Wilson

> "...he would give you almost everything, except himself."
> Franz Liszt on his friend and fellow composer, Frédéric Chopin

These ones do not throw out their scent like stars
but keep their fragrance inside
the way nectar is kept or inner happiness
and sometimes sorrow. When Chopin left
his native Poland for France, he was only twenty,
but musically he was complete. Inside of him—
the green and gold countryside,
the grain fields and forests of poplar, birch, willow,
and fir; the quiet streams, the voices
of his people, and always love that failed.
I listen to the nocturnes late in the evening
when the children are in bed, and I think of my mother
playing when I was young, I think of the most tender
memories of the slightest touch when he that I burned for
could not touch me. This is the purity of beauty
when we walk back over the vows and dangers,
the lost graces and temptations. Art makes a treaty
with this business of lost time and failed flesh.
The piano-strings comprehend; they too bore witness.
Each note placating what is neglected
and forgotten. The night-jasmine climbs vine-like
over the walls of the house as the keys descend
and settle. Near Warsaw, a man slight and elegant,
draws on his white gloves and boards the coach
for Paris. He doesn't look back. With modest self-assurance
he works those melodies that idle in his head.

# Comprimario

Jeffrey Levine

Chopin decided to travel blind.
What use are maps to someone who knows
his place does not know him? Let me explain.
The words "his place does not know him"
so beguiled Chopin that he whispered them
again and again, his right hand resting
on the keyboard. Suddenly illuminated,
he saw phrases enfold around the broken
edges of arpeggios, around scales scattered
like dried sea grass in the tidal pools—
away from the guesthouse with its strings
and hammers, far from his bedroom
with its southern light.

From his villa in Mallorca Chopin wrote,
"I caught cold in spite of the heat, palms, figs,
and the three most famous doctors on the island.
One said I had died, the second, that I am dying,
the third that I shall die."

When one is ready to leave, even a single
wooden spoon is enough to stir the world.
Add a colander, a perfect pairing knife,
or row upon row of ivory keys, tempered
and sweet, the heart wills itself to break.

# A Letter from Countess Wodzińska to her Daughter Maria, Winter, 1835

Tammy L. Tillotson

Bless me! Dear Maria, you are misled!
I am not particularly disposed
to find ill favor with Mr. Chopin,
yet I have some doubt he would afford you
all the comforts and all the privileges
which any home can give. Yes, it is in
several points to me offensive and
I do have my strong objections to it.
While I should be as glad as any a
mother would be to see her daughter wed
I must confess to being persuaded
to but ask for nothing more than to be
respectably removed of fear from this
engagement. Fear, not a selfish caution,
but a decision as not deserving
haste and as my sensible belief is
one of prudence which hopes that winter's end
will bring his health in good situation.
*As everything depends on that*, my dear,
you should be pretty well off when you are
gone away and I dare say we shall not
have such things of worry to distress us.

# A Letter from Maria Wodzińska to F. Chopin, September, 1836

Tammy L. Tillotson

My dearest Fryderyk,

My heart is heavy with sorrow!
But it is at my family's instruction
to profess the feeling of how impossible it is,
despite your efforts and sacrifices,
for me to truly accept your marriage proposal.
While my heart would like nothing more,
I see no personal advantages for either of us to refute this
direction.
Alas! With all the reasoning, my heart is quite worn out!
Though I may be talking idly, I have quite given up on dancing.
It is with tears in my fingertips that I continue in my playing,
as mechanically as the sun rises and sets,
while the ivory song of the moon never
chances to take its leave without me.
Father and Mother assure me there are many things
taken into account, however, I am determined
my family's direction is honorable and not designed
to seem prejudiced toward you.
I beg your pardon, for when my short answer
cannot be "I do" it is but cruelly in bidding you,
all my love and adieu.

Yours affectionately,

Maria

# A Letter from Fryderyk Chopin to Himself, September, 1836

Tammy L. Tillotson

Pray, what fair love will now not chance to grow?
Be my heart a weed of fair health withheld,
God hath exposed to every winter snow?
Oh, wretched, wretched bones! My fate expelled!
Yay, to be a cloud, cursed not as the moon!
To briefly greet her rising sun and be
a pillow on her setting bed! My tune
might then not seem as such great a pity.
No small tone could have been more desired
as had my pleasure acquainted with it.
Lovely a bloom be a rose inspired,
which so strangled a weed would not befit.
Yet, I as the weed, alone in the dark,
waltz to compose of her beauty's rare spark.

# Second Movement

Kathi Stafford

Maria Wodzińska:
*moja bieda*—my sorrow.
Words Chopin wrote
when he placed the letters from Maria
in an envelope.
Waltz in A-flat major.
The girl he kept yearning for—
the Polish girl
but he was too sick to marry her
oh, but not too sick to have the affair
with Sand

Poor girl wondering why Chopin
was off in Paris.

Pretending she was the inspiration
but really it was his own recollection.

The etudes, the preludes. She stopped
everything when he reached
the loud parts, the passages
that hurt her bones
until she knew her place—
phantom vessel,
banished.

# Twenty Six

## Beata Poźniak Daniels

1:26 a.m.
Young paradise of embarrassed eighty eight black
and white stars, full of life and light. They watch me,
enjoying their own fullness
and harmony of touch.
A peaceful-sleepy-dark chord holds my fingers tightly.
Warm wind tries to escape, the dancing
quarter notes leave,
improvising a new pattern,
simply playing hide and seek.
Breeze.
Surrendering.
A nocturne cries its name in the distance,
a mournful owl.
Suddenly, in a flash
of Marienbad my heart is drumming away.
The rhythm is carried by its movement and sound.
Fingers, toes are tingling still.
A bird that flies by
breaks the mood with two plus six repetition.
All parts of my body are opening to a new song,
a new symphony of thoughts. The music in me
grows fuller as the stars fade.
Disappear. I'm peeking out of my shell.
The illusion fades away
with the night. New sonatas of thoughts are born
and ready for the journey.
Dawn is just minutes away.
Madame Sound takes my hand. I am.
I am twenty six years old.

> Note: Marienbad is the location of Chopin's meeting with Maria Wodzińska, whose parents forced her to reject his marriage proposal. He was 26 years old.

Frédéric-François **CHOPIN**, compositeur
né à Zelazowa-Wola en 1809, mort à Paris en 1849.
Oeuvres : des Valses, des Fantaisies, des Scherzo,
des Nocturnes, des Préludes, la marche funèbre,
etc.

French postcard with Chopin's portrait and information about his life and works (wrong date of birth). Carte Postale, Edition Heintz-Jadoul, ca. 1900. Maja Trochimczyk Collection

# Chopin and Sand

Austin Alexis

*for Frédéric Chopin, 1810—1849*

A man coughing-up blood
on a white keyboard.
A woman taking care of him.
A woman adding a man
to her case, her collection
and at last having something to do:
a person who becomes an activity.

He lives in her shawl.
He lives on her shelf.
She frowns, afraid he might chip
or crack in two or scar.
He lives in her nest.
She is all leaves.
She is plenty of twigs.

His fingers sing for her;
they chirp; they fly.
She is the maple his claws grip,
the branch he needs
in order to soar.

He desires her as she longs for him.
They are as far apart
as petals of a single rose.

# Chopinesque

## Helen Graziano

As chords are to harmony
Chopin is to ripples
piano keys—eternal music flows from his pen
Even a tarantella—a wild
tumultuous dance for gypsies
France applauded
the Polish prodigy

As mouth is to silken skin,
his fingers tapped the ivories, touched
lightly first, then with force on a baby grand.
Chopin wrote—
deftly rising chords
into a crescendo.
As crystal is to clear
he composed
a river of romance to revel in.

George Sand, his Cleopatra,
 vixen and angelic muse.
He trusted her feminine
mystique
clad in slacks.
An intimate expression of joy—
liberated woman.
Sensual, frail man—Chopin.
Nuances in etudes, preludes, nocturnes,
better than any CD you can burn!

As bread is to life—
Free love. Now a dark–eyed star in composer's heaven.
Chopin—Sand, infamous—a duet.

Postcard of sick Chopin playing piano, based on a painting by Fr. Ulreich. Wiener Kunst series. Vienna: BKWI (Bruder Kohn), ca. 1900-1910. Maja Trochimczyk Collection.

# Chopin in Mallorca

Lusia Slomkowska

His hands were eloquent, though they trembled
During those days, nights at Valldemosa.
Living in an aging monastery, between the ledge
And the sea, he was without curls and white
Gloves and pale as a dinner plate,
And always longing for sounds of Paris,
But heard only the waves, their dissonant
Cries as they rose in thin wrists,
Fell into white knuckles.
He saw himself drowning in a torrent
Rising from the shore, beating at the door,
Until notes came falling from his poised hand
Onto the stark page in that very strange
Place that was precarious, eloquent, trembling.

# Winter in Majorca

Erika Wilk

promising
months of calm allow
inspiration to soar

it was not to be

for two agonizing weeks
his piano held at customs
lack of money
the offense

fury, frustration
wracked his spirit
until George Sand
paid for its release

once reunited he poured
his passion unto paper
although frail and ill
he gave his all

and gifted us with
most memorable music
preludes, a ballade, a scherzo
the Polonaise in C Minor

it WAS meant to be

# Discord

Martin Willitts, Jr.

1. Chopin to George Sand, 1847

The delicate touch you felt on your neck
is the same as on a piano, with the same lyrical rush,
the music of leaves in the resolute winds.
It is the same idiomatic language of geese leaving.
My heart has the same feeling, restless, yearning.
When I play a rondo, no one can hear the silence after.
I leave these early movements behind
like I must leave you.
Some things are finished when they are finished.

I thought of returning to you.
I hesitated at your window.
I knew if you saw me with that melodic look you have,
it would enrapture me.
Our bodies would become counterpoints.
But it would be fragmentary motifs. Textural nuances
of what used to be.

Our love was illicit, some say.
I say, it was melodic, rhythmic, and full of music.
Our love was repetitions of a single note.

You criticized me for my primitive sense of form
when we would lie in bed, soaked in harmonic intonations.
You were right about me as well as everything else.
I cannot help being in the soundscape of textures,
in the lightness of sound, in the last moment leaving you.
For life is opening one door and descending unknown stairs.

## 2. George Sand to "beloved little corpse"

You could not stand a woman who did not act like a woman
except in bed. Even then you were horrified
by the idea a woman could enjoy passion.
What were all those compositions of love-soaked music then?

You were not my first lover and you will not be my last.
A woman should pick and choose who will enter her bedroom.

You shake your head, expecting me to fall for your music like
others.

A woman cannot be a slave to men.
You will not allow us to be equal.
So what choice do I have?
What choice does any woman have?

I changed my name so I could publish what scandalizes you.
Women have a right to sincere love and I will write about it.
I shall write about my desires and disappointments.
I will not miss you. I will only find another.

What have you done recently?

Note: "Beloved little corpse" was her name for Chopin due to his numerous sicknesses.

# Chopin's Sorrow

### Georgia Jones-Davis

Sorrow I love
more than any woman

So do not run your fingers
along my skin
countess
touch me
with white gloves
or I will break
like a minor chord

Polish, French, man, woman
I speak none of these languages
only that of rain and moonlight

Sex will kill me
with its gabardine trousers
cigars and gaudy novels
slashed ribbon of arguments
must of unmade beds

The other night
in the Salle Pleyel
the moon
her full face composed
edged close to the windows
to listen

I kiss her holy white dust
I press my lips to the purity
of her bloodless devotion

A photograph of Chopin in 1849, the year of his death.
Unknown photographer. Postcard printed in New York,
ca. 1910. Maja Trochimczyk Collection

# Goodbye to Poland

Laura L. Mays Hoopes

What is that thread of sadness woven under the rich arpeggios
and brilliant chords? I hear the wailing and the breast beating
I hear growling dogs, the clashing swords and guns booming
I hear the anguish of Poland from your soul.
Justyna must have held your hand as you explored
her homeland, adopted by your French father,
the rich greens and golds of the country village
the hum and buzz of the cultured Warsaw.

But when opportunity beckoned there, you had to flee,
to move to France, to speak its garbled tongue
to make the matrons of society moan with delight
at your brilliant salon performances.
Composing Polonaises and Mazurkas took you back
for hidden visits to Żelazowa Wola woods,
to places you alone could perceive, to the Poland
of your dreams and wishes, now forbidden.
And that deep pain in the chords drew the ladies.
Listening, they flocked to you for the honey
with a trace of tears in it, how they hovered for
your melodies and wanted your company.
But inside, the disease of your time, the sneaking germ
the tuberculosis, the consumption, the lung decay
had you in its talons and pulled you down slowly
inexorably, however high your music soared.
And at the end, your sister, not your sweet ingénue,
nor George Sand your sophisticated intellectual lover,
stood by your bedside to help you breathe
as you finished your short life's Minute Waltz.

# Love Letter to Chopin

Carol J. Jennings

At thirteen, I fell in love with you,
upon hearing the Nocturne in E-flat,
and practiced for five years
to play you with the right *legato* and *rubato*,
trusting you would listen from some
heavenly perch and send me
a sign of your approval. It never came,
so I moved on to Liszt, with whom
you also shared lovers, I have read.

I wonder about Camilla –
pianist, married to a piano maker,
three of your Nocturnes dedicated to her.
But did you love her and she you?
And did you tell her in words
or only through the melody?
For me, it would have been enough.

And the other women,
married, unmarried, countesses, princesses,
to whom you dedicated
waltzes, ballades, mazurkas, etudes –
were they lovers and muses,
or just pianists with the right touch?
And what about George Sand –
the love of your life, biographers write,
yet nothing is dedicated to her?

I have come back to you years later,
not with the passion of adolescence,
but the sensibilities of an older woman,
and a willingness to take romantic liberties.

# Death

# In Which Thackeray's Daughter Visits the Dying Chopin

George Bodmer

While she and her sister stayed in Paris with her grandparents,
Isabelle Thackeray,
no riding hood,
rides with her grandmother's Scottish friend,
carrying a bucket of food and wine to the impoverished musician—
up three flights,
his flat empty
save a piano and a few chairs—
The woman asks, "have you been eating, have you been sleeping?"
"No, but I've been composing," he answers triumphantly,
and plays the piano—
the child can't remember the music she heard that day
but recalls the old woman saying,
"That was Chopin, he won't be with us much longer"—
she recorded it in her Unwritten Memoirs
fifty years later,
a lifetime to understand genius and exile

# Last Words

Jennifer S. Flescher

There are conflicting stories about Chopin's last words.
*The earth is suffocating,* I heard somewhere.
*Swear to make them cut me open, so that I won't be*

*buried alive.* I prefer this to the music historian's claim
on NPR today, *Play Mozart for me.* Heading down
the hill last night, the light was low and bright

at my back– we see the sky as blue
because our eyes are sensitive to the fractured;
color cut open from the sun.

Ahead, a dark charcoal rendering of the future,
etched by the remnants and the ready to release –
an impression of the holding still.

Between the fair day and the storm, a tree glowed,
suspended by the slope
of the hill. You can't see the light,

buried in the day. *Maybe it was heaven,*
the music historian said. Mahler asked for Mozart too.
The tree glowed and glowed until what was coming came.

# October 17, 1849

Kenneth Pobo

You composed while coughing
up your lungs.  Death
dozed in a chair,

waited—slightly before two
in the morning, night's keys
went silent.  You never

made it to forty.
200 years, a portulaca
blossom opening

for an afternoon
only.  Music's bloom
lasts longer—is it

formed from equal parts
of joy and doom?  Tonight
a woman at a piano

plays with utter concentration,
your notes keeping her
alive.

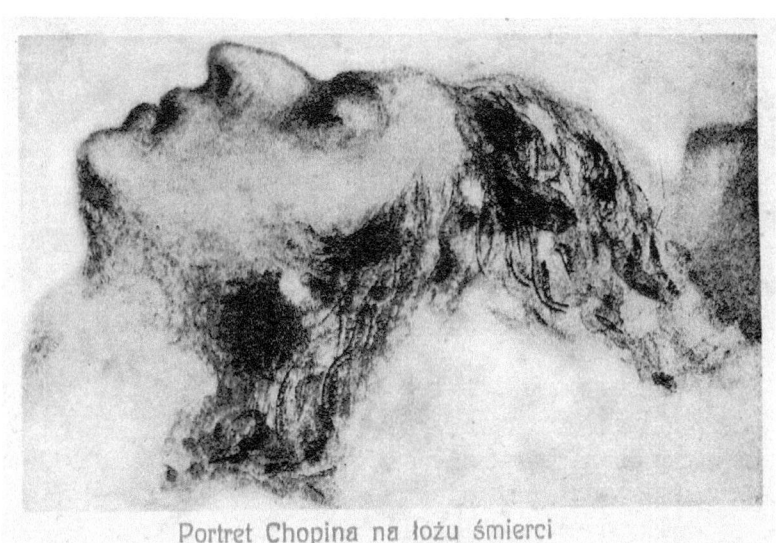

Postcard with a caption in Polish: "Portrait of Chopin on his death bed, according to a watercolor by T. Kwiatkowski." Published in Lwów: Nakł. Spółki Wydawniczej "Postęp," n.d., ca. 1910. Maja Trochimczyk Collection.

# Chopin's Death Mask

### Jean Baptiste-Auguste Clésinger, c. 1849

## Fiona Sze-Lorrain

I hear no mazurka
withhold his breath.

Lips bifurcate
where words are bait

to his last breath. Suppose
it travels. A letter going home.

A gaze moulds silence
inwards to the skull,

descends blackness, the soots of life.
Also the toxins

of his wretched romances.
Sunken eyes sag tempestuous

desires, nostrils shaped
as though shame is an odor.

Pungent debts stay registered,
they do not choke, they surface.

Think of the end
and resurrection.

One expression as dusk and light.

A visage salvaged
from erasure, like his signature

in courtesans' letters, a chosen exile,
the chromatic quavers:
        *Yours forever, mummifiedly yours.*

# At the "Hour of Twilight"

– after reading Franz Liszt on Chopin's death

Anne Harding Woodworth


Franz will write it all down:
that I swooned, that I asked for flowers
and music. Trouble is, I don't know any Franz.

Tens of friends waited
in the anti-chamber. Trouble is,
I don't have even four.

And a student held my hand,
because he wanted to return my affection
except that I've never had a student who loved me.

I do have a sister. I have two, but they wouldn't think
of being prostrate at my bedside.
So who will hold my hand?

Where is a Franz who will unabashedly
describe my pillow? my sweat? my bitter suffering?
the unknown shores where next I go?

Of course, it's true:
I don't believe I'm going anywhere,
nowhere beyond nothing, that is.

Sing, Countess. Sing, my compatriot.
Trouble is, I'm not Polish. I don't know any singers,
at least not one who can attain profound pathos.

And there's no one to roll the piano I don't own
to my bedroom door. Oh, Liszt, where are you?
I am coughing so. And the pain . . .

And the love . . .
Where is *my* Franz who will record
the cliché of a final agony?

Postcard *Chopin's Last Chords* based on a painting by J. Mecina Krzesz,
*Les derniers accords de Chopin*, Vienna: BKWI (Bruder Kohn),
c. 1900-1910. Maja Trochimczyk Collection.

# Everlasting Love

Erika Wilk

> *For where your treasure is, there will your heart be also*
> *Matthew VI:21*

His heart removed
preserved in brandy
taken to Warsaw
in his beloved Poland
his empty body buried in Paris
nearly three thousand people came to his funeral
but she—George Sand—did not attend
estranged by then
their long, turbulent relationship
came to a bitter end the year before
he suffered deeply
loosing her
distraught, of frail health, alone
he died
leaving an immeasurable void
still felt
by all of us

Warsaw has his heart enshrined
the world his music
then, now, forever

# Frozen Flowers

## Radomir Vojtech Luza

black and white flossing the bones of your fingers like melancholy does rain

there in that back room you work tearing lungs from lies into d flats and a destiny only your dilapidated daredevil dingo heart can find in the

underbelly of you and me the paralyzed and lonely those who have given up and never started know you chopin like a brother like that opera you could

not start because it was already finished that trip to scotland a message

you did not open until too late until satan had you wrapped around his tomato patch those forgiven hands at side when eyes closed and the music

was lifted to a dead world already sunburned by genius

# Playing

# We Speak Chopin

Marilyn N. Robertson

Once the piano seemed
an instrument most pedestrian,
though I did love to let
my fingers chase like rabbits
up and down the keys
playing inventive Bach.
Then I took a risk, turned
to Chopin, untangled knotted
chords, mastered fields of flats
and groves of spiny sharps,
smoothing over rough spots,
laying down the mental tracks.

Now the old piano's found
its own true voice. I am an actor.
The piano plays my part.
We speak Chopin. He demands,
I assert. He demurs, I linger
as if caught up in a dream.
Notes cast prism lights across
the walls, a drama in Technicolor,
my breath withheld.

# Chopin and I

## Mira N. Mataric

no need for others
though
Tchaikovsky, Schubert, Brahms,
Wienawsky, Grieg and Paderewsky
played their role

after the war at eleven I get a piano
start to climb cliffs with my bare fingers
through scales, arpeggios and small etudes
sadly distant from Chopin

then Beethoven—*Für Elise*—
a milestone and wink of encouragement

Chopin still unreachable
I listen hour after hour
to Rubinstein and only Rubinstein
no one else is right for Chopin and me

I study history and geography
rivers places and battles
romantic
but splattered with blood
(Chopin and I share a revolutionary streak)

memorizing math formulas
I am sprinkled with the filigree froth
of mazurkas
drowned in waltzes' passion

tormented souls Chopin and I
discover love and pain

his fragile body dies his soul finds peace
music cuts deeper and stays in me

I announce to my mother
no more piano lessons
her eyes darken with a new expression
I don't understand
something sinks…in me…in her…
and stays unresolved
like a dead child in a live womb

my grief explodes years later crying
why haven't you forced me
beat me
if necessary
to stay with the piano

her eyes fill with anguish
and something else

years pass
I listen to Chopin and Rubinstein
marry and have a daughter
she plays arpeggios and *Für Elise*
on my aging patient piano

in huge wave of pride and satisfaction
I blend with my mother
(now embalmed in sleep)

when my daughter quits piano
I agree
no questions asked

hurriedly leaving the room
so she cannot see my eyes
oh mother
now I know

time goes by
my grand daughter plays *Für Elise*
on a new shiny piano
I enjoy the moment
that cannot last

at peace alone
no matter who plays Chopin
I hear the ultimate version
of my lifelong dream of perfection
with Frédéric.

# Chopin and Church

Donna L. Emerson

I felt holy at twelve when I fainted in church,
three different Sundays. Dad carried me out
like Clara in *Heidi*.
Twelve was, I hoped, a holy number.

Sunday after another Saturday playing
Chopin for my piano teacher Mr. Ribble
as he cried in the church basement,
one light on to save electricity.

At first I thought my playing made him cry.
I pulled in my stomach and tried
to make every note ring.
Then he told me it was Chopin. He died young.

Dark everywhere there, I couldn't see between
the primary school chairs and the barred
windows to the street. I read all about Chopin,
the story above each piece. Even in the *Americana*

*Encyclopedia*, about leaving his native Poland,
his tuberculosis that made me think
of Cornel Wilde as Chopin in a movie, blood
on his white handkerchief,

George who didn't sound like my mother
or anyone I knew. I began to worry.
Chopin worried about Poland. I worried about
Chopin. And Poland. Sometimes coughing, too.

Do people still get tuberculosis? Chopin died
when he was thirty-nine, Mr. Ribble said,
the same age as Mr. Ribble's father, who
died twenty years ago. Mr. Ribble worried

all the time. We passed over the *Prelude
in C Minor*. Just waltzes, etudes. He wouldn't
let me play the funeral march. Chopin was the first
person I ever felt mixed up about. Then I wanted

to help him. I wouldn't have taken him to Majorca
where it rained all the time. George Sand thinking
mostly of herself. When Mr. Ribble left the church
I stopped piano lessons. My friend Barbara said
since I was now thirteen, maybe I knew enough.

# Posthumous

## Charlotte Jones

My sister's favorite was Chopin.
Mine, Bach.
He's baroque, she'd charge,
meaning broken.
Choppin'-sticksin! I'd retort,
then we'd laugh and play *Chopsticks*
until our parents hollered for us to stop.

Older, more talented,
the perfect-bitch-with-perfect-pitch
tried to convince me Chopin had more soul.

Then she died.
Unexpectedly.
Way too young.
Just like Chopin.

For twelve years,
the instrument
in my own home sat mute.
Any piano, too painful.
Too I-could-see-her-sitting-there.

A year ago, I took up piano again,
even practicing scales this time around,
longing for the day my
fingers could touch Chopin.

Last week, my first:
Waltz in A Minor
(Op. Posthumous).
So appropriate.

Now I understand what my sister meant:
the haunting gypsy melody,
the romance of running from life,
my face, tear-stained as I practice.

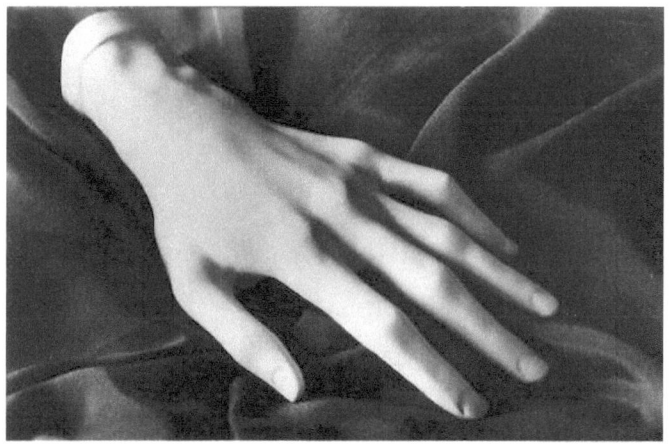

Postcard of a model of Chopin's hand by Augusto Clepenger.
France, ca. 1910. Maja Trochimczyk Collection.

# Impressions – Mario's Chopin

Lois P. Jones

*For Mario Feninger*

There is periwinkle—
a sky that Edith drags

at the hem, warm yolk
of a Cairo sun you brought

with you to Paris. The way
your fingers pull down the rain

when a boulevard aches.
Summers in Szafarnia,

where light is river waltz;
the mist that covers

our ankles. Snowflakes
are silent coins,

the nightscape of nocturnes.
Your hand at the small of my waist.

# Alicia Plays Chopin

Susan Rogers

--Susan Rogers

Chopin is at the piano—He plays a casual improvisation, then stops. "'Go on, go on,' exclaims Delacroix, 'That's not the end!' (Chopin explains,) 'I'm trying to find the right colour, but I can't even get the form...' 'You won't find the one without the other,' says Delacroix, 'and both will come together.' 'What if I find nothing but moonlight?' 'Then you will have found the reflection of a reflection.' Suddenly the note of blue sings out, and the night is all around us, azure and transparent. Light clouds take on fantastic shapes and fill the sky".
—George Sand, from *Impressions et Souvenirs*

## Alicia Plays Chopin

She is small boned,
with delicate skin—
English roses on white
and little for her age, which is eleven.
She looks to be no more than six or seven.
She sits upon my piano bench
as if it were her private chair
and tries to reach the pedals.
I have asked her to play
*Fantasie Impromptu*
because she says she can.

But seeing her sitting stiff and pale,
thin fingers ready on the keys,
her long, auburn, wavy hair
covering a sky blue cotton dress
like ringlets on a china doll,
my heart misgives.
Chopin?

Even though it is my birthday
I turn away, rethinking my request.
Suddenly, a note of blue sings out
and George Sand enters my piano room.
I hear her call the name
"Frédéric" and then "Eugene."
She says, "Night is all around,
azure and transparent," then she gestures
to the window and the moon.
As if in a dream, I see shapes of clouds
gather in the pictured blue.
Spinning notes into a conjured sky,
a fantasie impromptu sweeps
liquid music into being.
Born of nothing more
than moonlight from another time,
shadows, colors, waves of sound
rising in imagined love,
Chopin floods into the room
above the keyboard rushing, falling:
a passionate design.
It is just as Delacroix had said—
the right color and the right form
come together at the same time.
I find myself echoing his words,
when the last note of blue has gone
and only the sky blue dress remains,
imploring, "It's not the end—
Go on, go on."

# In the Music Stanzas

## Martin Willitts, Jr.

*For Chopin and my father who made me play his music*

    1.

Touching a lover, like a harpsichord,
two or three melodies, simultaneously,

is the same as chickadees locating each other
in woodland thickets,
both are the fugue, lost then found
in the acrobatics of love


    2.

presence is felt
when something is so immense
it is the song of the mockingbird
searching for the last note,
wing-flashing during courtship
feeling the wind bringing the voice within


    3.

a person cannot find peace
in snow on branches
like notes in a stanzas
are flights of birds into heaven.

Postcard *Chopin's Last Chords*, based on a painting by A. Setkowicz, *Ostatnie akordy Chopina / Chopinovy Dozvuky / Chopin's Letzte Akkorde / Chopin ejjeli dala.*Kraków, ca. 1900. Maja Trochimczyk Collection.

# Exiles (3)

Sheila Black

No Frenchman would be so well educated
with so little to show, you said. Your sister still
had her piano. Your mother her shelf of
Russian novels. She had studied with the greatest
orthopedic surgeon in Moscow. Strong hands, she told me,
splaying them on the table. Her daughter's
hands. In the empty apartment, your
sister played Chopin. Rain falling in Poland, rain falling
on the island of Majorca where the composer coughed and
bled and George Sand made poultices of thyme
and wild onions to assuage the hole in his lungs,
a bloodied lace and traces of music peeling
through windows. *The place where I have no nation,
the place where I have no history.* Only this sound
lingering in the hallways so that a woman going
out to the market pauses at the elevator. She does not hear
it, she only knows she remembers the marbles
she had as a child, little balls of clay and colored glass.
They knocked together on the dirt, and she
watched them with a fierce delight, mourning them,
one by one, when they were lost.

# Chopin in Ohio

## Donna L. Emerson

Fryderyk Chopin lived with us.
Mother played his dancing nocturnes,
mazurkas and waltzes every week.

I struggled to learn them, grateful
when a few bars became familiar.
When my piano teacher gave me

an entire book of Chopin, I gobbled
up all his story, his young picture,
first compositions.

How delicate and complex he was,
able to make melodies like Mozart,
flying us to heaven with grace notes.

How much he felt the conflicts
in Poland, how sad to leave his
country, like we had to leave Ohio

for Pennsylvania. How much
I became jealous of George Sand,
a kind of woman I did not grasp,

and when I played *the Raindrop
Prelude, in D-flat Major*, I cried for all
his rainy days in Majorca. Did he know

like Keats, that death was coming?
Could he push all his love and music
into his short life? Surrounding ourselves

with Artur Rubinstein in concert became
our consolation, hearing over and over, all
of Chopin as we sat in our new tract home.

# Listening

# Portrait of a Lady

T. S. Eliot

> *Thou hast committed--*
> *Fornication: but that was in another country*
> *And besides, the wench is dead.*
> *The Jew of Malta.*

I.

Among the smoke and fog of a December afternoon
You have the scene arrange itself--as it will seem to do--
With "I have saved this afternoon for you";
And four wax candles in the darkened room,
Four rings of light upon the ceiling overhead,
An atmosphere of Juliet's tomb
Prepared for all the things to be said, or left unsaid.
We have been, let us say, to hear the latest Pole
Transmit the Preludes, through his hair and finger-tips.
"So intimate, this Chopin, that I think his soul
Should be resurrected only among friends
Some two or three, who will not touch the bloom
That is rubbed and questioned in the concert room."
--And so the conversation slips
Among velleities and carefully caught regrets
Through attenuated tones of violins
Mingled with remote cornets
And begins.
"You do not know how much they mean to me, my friends,
And how, how rare and strange it is, to find
In a life composed so much, so much of odds and ends,
(For indeed I do not love it ... you knew? you are not blind!
How keen you are!)
To find a friend who has these qualities,
Who has, and gives
Those qualities upon which friendship lives.

How much it means that I say this to you--
Without these friendships--life, what cauchemar!"
Among the windings of the violins
And the ariettes
Of cracked cornets
Inside my brain a dull tom-tom begins
Absurdly hammering a prelude of its own,
Capricious monotone
That is at least one definite "false note."
--Let us take the air, in a tobacco trance,
Admire the monuments
Discuss the late events,
Correct our watches by the public clocks.
Then sit for half an hour and drink our bocks.

II.

Now that lilacs are in bloom
She has a bowl of lilacs in her room
And twists one in her fingers while she talks.
"Ah, my friend, you do not know, you do not know
What life is, you should hold it in your hands";
(Slowly twisting the lilac stalks)
"You let it flow from you, you let it flow,
And youth is cruel, and has no remorse
And smiles at situations which it cannot see."
I smile, of course,
And go on drinking tea.
"Yet with these April sunsets, that somehow recall
My buried life, and Paris in the Spring,
I feel immeasurably at peace, and find the world
To be wonderful and youthful, after all."
The voice returns like the insistent out-of-tune
Of a broken violin on an August afternoon:
"I am always sure that you understand
My feelings, always sure that you feel,
Sure that across the gulf you reach your hand.

You are invulnerable, you have no Achilles' heel.
You will go on, and when you have prevailed
You can say: at this point many a one has failed.
But what have I, but what have I, my friend,
To give you, what can you receive from me?
Only the friendship and the sympathy
Of one about to reach her journey's end.
I shall sit here, serving tea to friends...."
I take my hat: how can I make a cowardly amends
For what she has said to me?
You will see me any morning in the park
Reading the comics and the sporting page.
Particularly I remark An English countess goes upon the stage.
A Greek was murdered at a Polish dance,
Another bank defaulter has confessed.
I keep my countenance, I remain self-possessed
Except when a street piano, mechanical and tired
Reiterates some worn-out common song
With the smell of hyacinths across the garden
Recalling things that other people have desired.
Are these ideas right or wrong?

III.

The October night comes down; returning as before
Except for a slight sensation of being ill at ease
I mount the stairs and turn the handle of the door
And feel as if I had mounted on my hands and knees.
"And so you are going abroad; and when do you return?
But that's a useless question.
You hardly know when you are coming back,
You will find so much to learn."
My smile falls heavily among the bric-à-brac.
"Perhaps you can write to me."
My self-possession flares up for a second;
This is as I had reckoned.
"I have been wondering frequently of late

(But our beginnings never know our ends!)
Why we have not developed into friends."
I feel like one who smiles, and turning shall remark
Suddenly, his expression in a glass.
My self-possession gutters; we are really in the dark.
"For everybody said so, all our friends,
They all were sure our feelings would relate
So closely! I myself can hardly understand.
We must leave it now to fate.
You will write, at any rate.
Perhaps it is not too late.
I shall sit here, serving tea to friends."
And I must borrow every changing shape
To find expression ... dance, dance
Like a dancing bear,
Cry like a parrot, chatter like an ape.
Let us take the air, in a tobacco trance--
Well! and what if she should die some afternoon,
Afternoon grey and smoky, evening yellow and rose;
Should die and leave me sitting pen in hand
With the smoke coming down above the housetops;
Doubtful, for quite a while
Not knowing what to feel or if I understand
Or whether wise or foolish, tardy or too soon...
Would she not have the advantage, after all?
This music is successful with a "dying fall"
Now that we talk of dying--
And should I have the right to smile?

# Concert at Chopin's House

Margaret C. Szumowski

The people are waiting, waiting
for a cabbage, a cup of flour.
They look so tired – Krisha, big-bellied
with little Ala struggling
in her arms. But for their guests

they find fresh bread, blueberries,
a glass of tea. New city, Nova Huta,
so far from forest, so far from sea. Inside
a plant defies gravity, spreads over the wall
like tapestry in a medieval castle.  Uncle

Bronislaw is always laughing, always fishing;
everyone says he will die fishing. Today
there is a big salmon for lunch. Three generations
in a tiny apartment, no place to rest. But every
Couch becomes a bed: even strangers find rest

here. We see the glacial lake, the virgin
forest. My husband is a bridegroom again,
flowers in his hand. Gypsies play violins
in the streets of Gdansk.  On Sundays

at Chopin's house something spills over, overflows
from the bungalow into the rose garden, into the hovering
trees. As we ride back towards Warsaw, children's lips

and hands purple with berries. Today
the opera is full, today the churches
are bursting.

# Postcards of Home and Homesick

Diane Shipley DeCillis

I stand alone in my yard in Detroit
listening to Chopin and eating a peach.

> The City of Lights, shadowed
> by the Carpathian Mountains,
> the salt of a Baltic breeze,
> did little to soothe the ache
> of home. His postcards—
> polonaises and mazurkas—
> cannons hidden among roses.

The peach smells like a nocturne.
I hold the pit, plant a peach tree
in my palm, imagining the soil
where roots travel and tendrils clench.

> His music, filled with marches,
> the sound of footsteps heading
> home. Ballades and preludes,
> written in a thousand shades of gray.

I envy how roots trust the darkness,
tap root, heart root, burrowing
through layers of silt and clay
as if propelled by a knowledge
of bedrock, of home.

> Before his burial in Paris, he asked
> to have his grave sprinkled with Polish
> soil and his heart removed, sent back

to Warsaw—his sister carrying the red bloom
of it in a glass urn, a rose crawling
the white picket fence of his childhood.

In my yard, my heart
is a seed that grows in
the shadows of home, the place
I first saw the sun, my face
always turning in that direction.

A reward card published by Theodore Presser & Co in Philadelphia,
Pennsylvania, ca. 1900, to be given by music teachers as a reward
for their students. Maja Trochimczyk Collection.

# An American Hears Chopin

Sharon Chmielarz

We were in Kraków. A cold evening.
    His hand, warm in mine.
        We saw a flyer, a concert, Chopin.

Near Dom Polski. A second story. A small,
    square hall. I couldn't find it again.
        Not alone.

Every seat taken. The piano huge, awkward,
    old-fashioned the way it spoke
        two languages at once,

vows between hand and keyboard.
    One sings back a gasp,
        directs all regrets to lie still.

Bathed in music.
    We the bathers,
        the bathed.

Love making is a good sport,
    Shakespeare said.
        The end flowers into silence.

The last song.
    We sat side by side, silent.
        The room, loved till death.

# Chopin in North Dakota

Thom Tammaro

*—for Jay and Martha Meek*

I am in Grand Forks, North Dakota, where I have come to spend the day with friends. After an afternoon of good talk and wine, we decide on dinner at the Ramada Inn restaurant. The place is nearly empty, but there is a woman in an emerald sequined gown playing the piano. So, here we are in North Dakota, at the beginning of February, waiting for our dinners, listening to Marvin Hamlish and Barry Manilow and "You Light up My Life." The pianist's name is Loretta. She introduced herself between songs and said she takes requests.

So we drop a few dollar bills in the wide-mouth goblet and ask if she knows any Chopin. She seems delighted, says she hopes we won't mind if she plays them with a lounge tempo. "No problem," we say, and just as our meals are being served, we hear a Chopin Etude, and then another, and then Beethoven's "Für Elise."

Later that night driving home to Fargo, scanning the radio, I tune in a station that, to my surprise and joy, is playing a program of Chopin sonatas and nocturnes. Such luck! Maybe it is Chopin Day in North Dakota! And as I drive beneath the dark veil of prairie sky, I remember a day six years earlier, when I went in search of Chopin's grave on a rainy afternoon in early March in Père-Lachaise Cemetery in Paris. I was alone, walking the narrow footpaths, holding my unfolded cemetery map, when I heard the voices of two Americans behind me also looking for his grave, so I invited them to share my map, and we walked together is search of it. And when we found it, the father and his teenage daughter seemed so happy. I never asked their names. Fresh bouquets of flowers surrounded the base of the gravestone. Wet sheet music. A score from an Etude. A pair of ballet slippers. Two unopened letters postmarked from Poland. Two poems written in French between two sheets of plastic. Even a few black and white ivory piano keys that someone arranged atop the tombstone! I felt so happy in that moment in the rain in Paris at Chopin's grave!

Tonight, even though I am not standing in the rain in Père-Lachaise Cemetery in Paris, or sitting outside Café Karlsplatz in Vienna, near the house where Chopin once lived, sipping tea from a flowered porcelain cup, and listening to a string quartet with friends, I am happy driving alone along the dark edge of North Dakota after midnight, after listening to Loretta play Chopin at the Ramada Inn, looking up at the stars, feeling the music of friendship, the tempo of the moment carrying me along, the full moon suspended on the prairie horizon like a huge golden coin, lighting up my life all the way home.

Postcard with Chopin's tomb at the Père Lachaise cemetery in Paris.
Ca. 1900. Maja Trochimczyk Collection.

# Artsy Evening

Ryan McLellan

E Major magician,
Chopin, are you listening?

Downloaded your music
for free
because I heard
on Public Radio
that you were "bi-polar"

the clips from
your compositions were
convincing
enough
to spike an interest –
As we prepared
our veggie stir-fry,
she said,
"You seem really –
I don't know – down"
and I heard
a piano
amidst the crackling
of dinner, silverware,
an old LP
and the summer
heat –

# Chopin in Manchester

## Anna Maria Mickiewicz

He did not like the smog
He did not like the damp English weather
or overcrowded Manchester

Standing at the lake in Prestwich
I can feel his longing
far away from home

Music is dripping like rain from his thin fingers rapidly
in the Gentlemen's Concert Hall

Today
his statue is silent in Manchester
a frail figure
Is he missing the music or his homeland?

Until later
other fingers of another musician
in exile

Ryszard Bakst is playing Chopin

# Chopin in an Old Church

Rick Lupert

The pianist performs humble as a river
We are in one of Paris' oldest churches
built when the memory of Jesus was young
like America

You can hear every noise,
the scuffling of a foot
the scratching of my pen
the dueling concertos
from the piano
and someone's cell phone

The acoustics of a stone cathedral
make you feel like you're there

The pianist's fingers
are as confident as rain

# Flight to Seattle

Peggy Castro

Clouds bathed by the sun
Chopin's Preludes ringing in my ears
I soar into heaven
on angel wings
dusted with a bit of sorrow

A Soap Trade Card from Portugal by Claus & Schweder, ca. 1900. Caption: Sabonete - Celebridades - Fabrica de Productos Chimicos Claus & Schweder - Porto (Portugal). Maja Trochimczyk Collection.

# Chopin on the Radio

Ryan McLellan

on my way to work and on the
radio as soon as I pull out
of the parking lot – dainty

key tapping mixed with thunderous
dark chords, pounded with a
blacksmith's ferocity to the

summer sun; a call to peaceful
arms – turned up the music as I
drove past the gas station,

doing well but sometimes I feel
like a nocturne, a raga, a left-
hand turn with no directional –

sometimes I feel just fine and
I have no one to thank for it.

# Chopin in the Snow

## Helen Vandepeer

Outside, snow falls. I watch
silent, diaphanous crystals.

I'll not venture out today.
Chopin plays. It is Christmas time.

My man sleeps on the couch.
Our house is quiet and at peace.

Gracious it is, full of color,
flowers in every room.

Echoes of love and laughter fill
our cottage, their portions equal.

Chopin continues. The snow
whitens the landscape.

The beloved, blanket-covered one
sleeps on. Music tempo quickens.

Snow falls thicker, faster,
in amazing synchronicity with the notes.

Chopin's sweet melody plays on.
Such peace, such joy –

I retreat from the window.
Soup bubbles in a pot.

# He Sings Chopin, I Hum Brahms

Charlie Durrant

In afternoons
your heart sings Chopin
while I hurriedly hum—in Brahms notes
to lullaby away your sorrow.
You then sing Liszt;
meanwhile, my fingers fumble…
I try to play Rachmaninoff
while you rant Gershwin
all over the scales.
I, in turn, play Bach, then Tchaikovsky,
while you rant on…
Later,
we both settle on Beethoven,
so deep, only oceans
can bear the weight of our song.
I know you, My Love…
know you
like my fingers know an octave from a fifth.
I could play you like Mozart,
but I can't play you more lovely than you are.

So, on with our duet,
and when you cease to sing,
I, with a song half-formed in my throat
will thither on through winter,
singing Chopin
over broken keys,
while you, a phantom, strum Brahms
on my heart strings.

Postcard *Chopin Composing the Preludes*, based on a painting by
L. Balestrieli, *Les Preludes*. France and Russia: Lapina, ca. 1910.
Maja Trochimczyk Collection.

# Chopin, Sheep, Feet

Allison Campbell

Smashed between two piano keys,
I go to crawl out of this etude.
But another finger and another finger
moving Chopin, right before his death,
fast, sweaty Chopin face, fast, are there.
And I'm between keys again.

My feet drag, not in the drunk,
not in the happy from my last meal, ways.
They sulk, they pin, walk tip-toed in cement
blocks towards my decisions, remember
the past and want to keep on remembering,
no matter the rest of me. They are stubborn,
stubborn feet, think they have their own
body, forget they're connected, forget to go
and stay. They forget where they shouldn't.

Then bang! Bang! They make me dance.
Then, alright, they make me dance. By will
their own, without my help, they're MC Hammering
in the orchestra of my adulthood, they pounce
on every note, then again, I'm stuck
between piano keys, pushed by all kinds
of fingers, holding up over the rise and fall,
the crescendo that just happens
to be me flying up.

And actually, I was born up, just didn't notice
until it was too late to be of any use. But maybe
we're all born up, aren't we? At least we're born

up by ignorance of our place, where we sit
in the universe, and how we know
nothing of pride, nothing of shame.

Then the bossy ones. Our feet with their instincts,
always making salmon of us thinkers.
Say we are sheep, and you'll be right.
I should speak for myself when I confess
I'm a follower, a sheep, the worst kind of sheep.
Oh, to be a sheep, to need these hooves. Where today,
hooves? Where today? And they won't answer,
my feet, which happen to be hooves, because,
alright, I've admitted it, alright, I'm a sheep.

But I can bounce, oh, how I can bounce.
And don't get me started on the mountains.
Did I mention I was born up, that I'm moving
up, and up, that I was born there and didn't even
realize until it was too late, and I was already on
my way down, clutching, clutching
the outlines of great ideas.

I told the things I needed they could leave.
This way, they felt safe about staying.
When I explained this to a book once,
I explained it to the Count of Monte Cristo,
before I even flipped to page one I spilled it,
said, "Hey, Dumas, and everything you've written.
These are my feet, this is my need, and here is my silly
falling from where I didn't know I was. Up, up."

# Fifteen Ways of Hearing a Wind Chime

Marlene Hitt

I
In the midst of darkness
wind chimes are but shadow.
A light comes on.

II
Three tones are clear in shadow or in darkness.
The blaze of sun makes no change.

III
Children hide in deep grass
away from the breeze.
Chiming follows them
even to roots in the ground.

IV
If I could sing that sweetly
I would sing many notes.

V
A puppy yelps and yelps
cracking the silence.
The sound of wind chimes
strokes the afternoon.

VI
One January wind
ripped away the music.
Grasses wrapped around it
to keep it while it slept.

VII
The gardener saw the shine of notes
strings tangled under alyssum,
a wind chime broken.


VIII
What is in the magic
of these tones?
Three men contemplate.
Nine sounds blend,
an ensemble.

IX
At dawn, wind chimes hang golden,
mended and polished, sound like bells.

X
"Fats" blew hard,
his cheeks round as apples,
harder than wind.

XI
Small Sarah climbed the old trellis
to touch gold, to be a wind making
many notes. So lovely. Old wood bent
into a thump and a cry. Wind chimes
played a jumbled background,
round like small drums.

XII
Air vibrates from fine brass
into eardrums and through bone.
Lips smile and eyes close.

XIII
A new February butterfly
lights on that golden blossom.
Swings, carries away her own song.

XIV
A mother nurses her new baby
while they hear Nocturne in E flat Major
then the Prelude and a Waltz
before he falls asleep.

XV
A neighbor drives by, hip hop bass
shakes the ground. Chimes still sing
Their own wind song.

# Beauty

# When Isadora Duncan Danced Chopin

Mary Rudge

When you felt the waves crash through you,
storm which Chopin's music made,
barefoot you cresendoed across the floor;
as white foam flung in air from rock,
your veils swirled around our hearts
swept us ashore.

The pianist's fingers passionately
danced the keys.

You said you learned to move as water moves,
as moonlight in the toss of trees,
and all your body flow as music flows.

Your chosen partner in the dance—Chopin,
only his music, takes
you high upon the billowing tide,
transports us in your wake,

we see the swell as genius overpowers,
as note after note
the music's ocean like a lover comes,
lifts your arms and lets you go.

Note: Isadora first danced Chopin when she went to London, 1900, and when she returned to San Francisco in 1917, she created an all-Polish program with music by Chopin which she then took on tour to France. The Russian Prince, Peter Lieven, later wrote, "Isadora Duncan...was the first to dance the music and not dance to the music."

# The Last Dance

Davi Walders

We take our seats for The Royal Ballet's
Washington performance of "A Month
in the Country". We have come to hear
Chopin's music, to watch Alexandra Ansanelli's
Natalia, to be enchanted by Frederick Ashton's
choreography and a famous prima ballerina.

The program tells so little—nothing about
John Lanchbery's weaving three of Chopin's
compositions into one score for ballet, nothing
about Chopin's life when he composed his
Grand Fantasy in A Major, the Grand Polonaise
in E-flat Major, or variations on Mozart's
*Là ci darem la mano.* All we know is that Ashton

chose Chopin's music to lift Ansanelli into
Turgenev's long, shimmering summer afternoon,
an afternoon of love and loss. This performance
marks a loss, too, as the Royal Ballet returns to London,
and, as announced just before the curtain rose,
Alexandra Ansanelli will dance as prima ballerina
for the last time before retiring at twenty-eight.

We watch this last poetry of movement as each
musical gesture becomes a dance gesture,
as Ansanelli in white lace and tender harmony
bids a final farewell to her lover, her audience,
and Chopin, both ballerina and composer now
famous for sudden, unexpected changes of keys.

# Dance with Me

## Mira N. Mataric

wildflowers grass and bursting ripe berries
thorny sunrays piercing primordial trees
dew shimmering like innocent tears
grandma's linen and Belgian lace

fragrance of mazurka and yellowing quince
atop her credenza
the nocturne allures into the dream
brocaded ladies in powdered wigs
gliding waltzes like Gioconda's smile
a sprinkle of apple and cinnamon breeze
lullaby and touch of a gentle hand
nothing helps

fragile is the moment
infinite human pain
no words
no words
please
only music understands

Chopin

whom god loves dies young

# Chopin: Apples

Sharon Chmielarz

And what country hasn't he lived in,
his music chilling the listener's arms?

And when haven't his glissandos
spilled over history, the colossus

that upsets lives like apple carts?
Apples rolling over cobbles.

God-fall we think,
finding among the bruised,

a handful of sweet apples.
The easy thank you is listening

to someone playing at a window
in Warsaw, turning the rumble

of despair into a mazurka.
"Beloved little corpse," Sand called Chopin,

sitting beside him at the keyboard.
Her "angel." His music, his wings.

# It's Been a Tough Symphony Week

Katrin Talbot


Every night,
Chopin shoves us
against the wall
and tenderly asks
the same questions:

'Why didn't you . . . ?
Why did you . . . ?
And why didn't you . . . ?'
within the soliloquies
of the pianist

and our eyes moisten
as we try to
explain, defend, apologize,
with only seven bars to go
before we're at it again

But we can't take the Inquisition
personally, can we?

After all,
it's what he does best,
isn't it?

# Eat When Hungry, Sleep When Tired

– a Zen saying

Marian Kaplun Shapiro

and then there is Chopin, meandering
from five impossible flats to four sharps
as if each measure were a casual ripple
in a spring stream of melting centuries.
What are we to make of him? *Nocturnes*
unnecessary as diamond necklaces,
*fantasies* frivolous as sequined
ballgowns. His *preludes* sing us into the land
of sadnesses deeper than the deepest
snowdrifts. His *valses* whirl us into that
last dance of the evening. They hold
us to each other. They show us the fire-
fly, the precious light before light's out.
They teach us about breathing. When hungry,
eat. When tired, sleep.

Postcard with a portrait and signature
of Chopin, with an inscription in German at the back.
Dresden: Stengel & Co., ca. 1900-1910.
Maja Trochimczyk Collection.

# The Composer

> – after Chopin

Leonore Wilson

Imagine how it must be— so enamored of sound
   of your own blood-buzz that your body grows limp

under the weight; imagine in the languid heat of April,
    you are leaf-mold clinging to the animate

and the not-so animate, borderless, that which falls
   into your flesh, becomes you, as sugar dissolves

into tea or rum poured drop by drop upon the slice
   of lemon floating on the surface of the hot liquid

making it golden… imagine how every ping of noise
   must hurt as the first touch when sex became

new, how that touch was like the short blue flame
   on the stove that you wanted… oh to be all

mouth of sound like an infant sucking its fingers,
   to almost wrap yourself out of it, the hunger

like the inclined urn tipped over, even your pockets
   in their small corners have the pinprick of melodies

like anything that falls into a black hole and is eaten;
   you, too, are that tunnel where it all disappears,

you are that pinch of night, chink of the pleated shutter
   going up, bee of desire like a scratch on mahogany,

you are the scoop of gutter water in the palm, dumpy
    mouth of your mother, little dab of butter on the plate,

and she who washed the plate; how you hear your own
    skin where it nips too tightly under your ear, you are

the lovers' whisperings, their wits quickened by you
    who guard their secrets and don't feel jealous,

you know their mutterings are followed by the slice
    of the broad-bladed knife against the warm bread,

the kitchen noise itself like the snap of broken wood, or
    of hair unloosened, of the fall of the curtains

three floors up, of hands still wet with blood, the slightest
    thrill of the accidental or the skinny man's disinterest,

the bright pain of the priest clutching his collar, of door hinges
    and points of scissors and then the strong scent of laurel,…

# Beyond Utopia

## Radomir Vojtech Luza

it was paradise your mind the music the polish people and the potholes you

filled like a lord among the lorded the legs strong as airports the hands bedeviling as santas sleigh

and you there always possessing plundering piano the curves in the road never stopped you the fallen trees collected at your side like a master

of skies and a wizard of cries staring out of the window at himself at the end he probably thought of a concerto or introduction but the hands would

not and poland had lost the light the love the lunatic of their warsaw their reason for breathing empty skies and aborted thank yous

# Souvenirs

Oriana Ivy

When I left Warsaw that October
when white smoke threaded heaps
of blackened leaves,
I took with me no photographs.

I took a cheap old knife
"because you never know" –
my mother's first commandment.
Wartime. Apocalypse. The wolf

at the door. That knife, a coin,
and checkered pink pajamas
made of Egyptian cotton
are the three souvenirs I own.

The knife is all aluminum.
Its blade is chipped,
the handle flowers a gray blotch.
The knife hides the reflection

of the beige-brown linoleum
in our make-shift kitchen,
a walled-off end of the corridor
at the Nencki Biology Institute.

The blade encrypts an equation
for the arc of my father's hand
stirring oatmeal on a camping stove,
making me breakfast before school.

The coin paid streetcar fare.
With that coin I possessed the city,
even the Royal Gardens – the statue
of Chopin, the weeping willows,

the sundial and the marbles.
A worthless coin, an ironic symbol:
my young life was rich
in treasures that cannot be bought –

wild swans in flight
over a green Mazurian lake,
family stories drifting off, duels
and great love, barbed wire and fog.

My Warsaw pajamas,
mummified in stale creases,
could still keep me warm,
but California nights

are not cold enough
for such pharaonic cloth.
A coin that can buy nothing,
a knife that doesn't cut,

and antique pajamas –
that's my estate,
my sacred wealth,
the covenant I keep.

# The Sounds of Chopin: A Villanelle

## Kerri Buckley

Hearts open    like French doors       as Chopin plays
At his birth, cherry blossoms were splashed with snow
Entering sound    deeply changes       ways one prays

His concertos    have filled       cafes, chateaus, chalets
Inspiring toasts with brandy, champagne, or Bordeaux
Hearts are open French doors       when Chopin plays

Faces aglow, women wear taffeta, velvet,       brocades
Join men in bow ties, gloves, a man gleams in a tuxedo
Slipping into glissandos    changes how he deeply  prays

Intoxicating Nocturnes    brightly sets one's soul    ablaze
Chords slice air like fire batons atop the high crescendo
Hearts could burst    like French doors     if Chopin plays

Lovers' lips shine like sugar, chocolate,       cherry glacés
In hours most arrive, sweethearts steal away, dolce adagio
Entering melodies softly changes ways    a beloved prays

Composers' lives overflow in continuous,    sacred praise
Onstage below glimmer of candelabras, maestros glow
Hearts glisten, French doors wide open    as Chopin plays
Enter music to change all deep mystical ways one prays

# Fryderyk Speaks to George of the Sky

Elizabyth A. Hiscox

*"3784 Chopin" – small asteroid in main belt*

They've placed me in the vault:
fashioned me
near Jupiter and Mars;
fastened me to the side of old gods.

Power and War, my love,
a chaos created by moveable giants;
an uprising of stone circling itself
all orbital resonance and constant revolution.

Crowded together like notes
written in failing health.

I miss the way the earth broke
over itself each morning:
*tender eyedawn of aurorean love.*
Broke all of us.

Space, its extended nocturne
is a grand room, my love.
But, as with the past, there is no sound
– only music.

Note: Italicized line is from John Keat's "Ode to Psyche."
George Sand was the pseudonym for Chopin's one-time lover,
Amandine Aurore Lucile Dupin.

# Chopiniana

Emily Fragos

Those hermits in their caves with their violent, pleading loves,
their moist eyes, are real and understandable to me now.
Their caves are right here in the palm of my hand.

The furious world with its murmurs in white corridors,
its endless dying off, has moved into a deep, invisible room
where the occupants do nothing but stain and scratch the walls.

What remains moves fathomless and ravished, a Chopin of elation,
performing so easily what is impossible to do. I am relieved of the burden
of language and arriving and know for a fact that I need not speak.

World, I will not smile at you anymore. It is the dance in me, born--
quiver to cadence and every touch a wild tactility, the salty eye.

# CONTRIBUTORS

**MILLICENT BORGES ACCARDI's** writing awards include grants from the National Endowment for the Arts, the Barbara Deming Foundation, and the California Arts Council, as well as residencies at Yaddo, Jentel and Vermont Studio. *Nimrod, The Wallace Stevens Journal, Tampa Review,* and *Salt River Review*, are recent credits, and, in September 2008 she was a writer in residence at Fundación Valparaíso, an international arts residency located on the Mediterranean coast, in the old Moorish hill town of Mojacar, Spain.

**AUSTIN ALEXIS** has published poetry and fiction in *Barrow Street, The Journal* (Ohio State University Press), *The Pedestal Magazine, The Writer, Six Sentences, Tuesday Shorts,* the anthologies *Off the Cuffs, And We the Creatures, Empty Shoes* and elsewhere. His chapbook, *Lovers and Drag Queens,* was published by Poets Wear Prada. He received a Bread Loaf Writers' Conference Scholarship and a Millay Colony Residency Fellowship.

**LUCY ANDERTON's** first love is music, which, she hopes, shows up in her poetry. She plunks away at Chopin on the piano in the 500-year-old brothel which she is rebuilding in the south of France after being writer-in-residence for the Virginia Center for the Creative Arts in the same French town: Auvillar. Her poems have appeared in *The Iowa Review, AGNI Online, DIAGRAM, Barrow Street,* among others, and are forthcoming in the *From the Fishouse Anthology.* She also represented Chicago in three National Poetry Slams and was the Grand Slam Champion at the 2003 Taos Poetry Circus.

**SHEILA BLACK** is the author of a chapbook, *How to be a Maquiladora* (Main Street Rag Publishing, Inc., 2007) and two full-length collections, *House of Bone* (CustomWords Press, 2007) and *Love/Iraq* (CustomWords, November 2009). In 2000, she received the Frost-Pellicer Frontera Award, given to one U.S. and one Mexican poet living along the U.S.-Mexico border. Most recently, she was Visiting Professor of Poetry at New Mexico State University. She lives in Las Cruces, New Mexico.

**GEORGE BODMER** is a printmaker in Chicago and teaches children's literature at Indiana University Northwest.

**LIA BROOKS** has great difficulty thinking about anything else but poetry. When she isn't writing you'll usually find her with a nose in a book or somewhere outside walking, either in the woods or by the sea. Her work has been published in *Penumbra, South, Shadow Train, First Time, California Quarterly, Loch Raven Review* and various other print and online magazines and anthologies in the U.K. and the U.S. She was short-listed for the New Leaf Short Poetry Prize in 2007 and her work has been part of two ekphrastic events in collaboration with painters in California and Indiana. She is also a painter and resides in Southampton, England.

**KERRI BUCKLEY** is a poet, freelance writer, and artist from the Pacific Northwest. She grew up in Kansas City where her father played in an orchestra. She teaches classes on writing, art, and meditation, and has hosted

The Literary Cafe' Radio Show since March 2005. In addition to poetry and articles, she is writing a novel about the Pacific NW. She recently won First Place for her poem "The Man From San Jose," in the Inland Empire California Writer's Club Annual Poetry Contest. Her website is www.kerribuckley.com

**ALLISON CAMPBELL** received her Masters in Creative Writing from the University of Southern Mississippi's Center for Writers. Her work has most recently appeared in *Court Green, The Wine Enthusiast, Luna Park*, and is forthcoming in San Francisco-based *Big Bell*. She currently writes and teaches in Torreón, México.

**PEGGY CASTRO** has been writing poetry since she was 14; for ten very productive years she was a part of Pasadena Poets. Presently, she belongs to Kathabela Wilson's Cal Tech Poetry Club and to Southern California Haiku Association. Her greatest achievements are two lovely daughters and five wonderful grandchildren. Ms. Castro currently works for Pacific Clinics as a Case Manager.

**SHARON CHMIELARZ's** books include *Different Arrangements, But I Won't Go Out in a Boat, The Other Mozart* (made recently into a two-part opera) and *The Rhubarb King*. She's had poems published in magazines like *The Iowa Review, Prairie Schooner, The Laurel Review, The Hudson Review, Water~Stone, Great River Review, North Dakota Quarterly, Salmagundi* and many others. She's had one chapbook published, *A Stranger in Her House*. Two new books of poems are forthcoming from Loonfeather Press and Whistling Shade Press.

**VICTOR CONTOSKI** published five books of poetry (issued by New Rivers, Tellus, and Cottonwood), two books of Polish translations: *Unease*, translations of Tadeusz Różewicz, New Rivers; and *Planting Birches*, translations of Jerzy Harasymowicz, New Rivers. He also published numerous poems, translations, and reviews in various literary magazines. He is a professor emeritus at the University of Kansas, where he taught American literature and creative writing from 1969-2006. He is currently working on a long series of dream poems, of which "Chopin Nocturne" is one.

**CLARK CROUCH**, a prize-winning Cowboy Poet of Bothell, Washington, delivers the reality of the West through his western and cowboy poetry. His viewpoints and biases result from his youthful experience as a cowboy during the Great Depression and periods of drought. The author of six books of poetry, including *Western Images*, that won the 2008 Will Rogers Medallion Award for Cowboy Poetry and was named as one of the top five cowboy poetry books of 2008 by the Western Music Association. His most recent book, *Views from the Saddle*, was published in June 2009 by Western Poetry Publications.

Born in Gdańsk, Poland, **BEATA POŹNIAK DANIELS** is an acclaimed actress, artist, activist and poet. Best known for her role as Marina Oswald in Oliver Stone's *JFK*, she starred in over 30 film and TV projects internationally, including "Babylon 5," "Melrose Place," "Mad About You," "JAG," "Zlotopolscy" and other TV series in the U.S. and Poland. As an activist, she spearheaded passage of the first bill to recognize International Women's Day in the U.S. Poźniak's paintings and sculptures exploring the roles of women in society have attracted the attention of Los Angeles galleries. Her theater company, Theatre Discordia, has presented numerous avant-garde theater projects combining dance, magic, visual projections, and spoken word. www.beata.com

**JESSICA DAY** has previously been published in *Bi Any Other Name* and *Mare Nostrum*. She is a recipient of the Allegheny College Creative Writing Award and the Mary Rouvelas Short Fiction Prize. She is a founding member of an arts non-profit called the Heroes and a judge for the *Notes and Grace Notes* online publication. Jessica completed her MFA at the University of Washington and currently resides in Seattle.

**DIANE SHIPLEY DECILLIS'** poems have appeared or are forthcoming in *Nimrod International Journal, Connecticut Review, CALYX Gastronomica, Gargoyle, Phoebe, Poet Lore, Puerto del Sol, Rattle, Spillway, North Atlantic Review*, and other journals. She won the Crucible Poetry Prize 2005 and the 2005 MacGuffin National Poet Hunt and is co-editor of *Mona Poetica*, an anthology of poetry on the Mona Lisa published by Mayapple Press. She was nominated for a 2009 Pushcart Prize.

**LORI DESROSIERS'** chapbook of poetry, *Three Vanities*, was published by Pudding House Press in 2009. Her poetry has been published in *BigCityLit, The Smoking Poet, Concise Delights, Blue Fifth Review, Ballard Street Poetry Journal, November 3rd Club, Common Ground Review*, Gold Wake Press' five-poem mini-chapbook series and others. She is the Editor of *Naugatuck River Review*, a journal of narrative poetry, and also publishes *Poetry News*, an online newsletter of poetry-related events in the CT/Mass. region. She earned her M.F.A. in Creative Writing/Poetry from New England College.

**CHARLIE DURRANT** is the founder and director of *PIGGY INK*, or *Poets Inking for the Global Good*. She was born, raised, and still resides in rural Idaho. There on her family's thousand-acre farm, she learned to appreciate the subtle beauties of the seemingly ordinary, like laying-hens, dairy cows, feed crops, sage brush, beans, potatoes, and whatever else ended up on their doorstep to raise. She was born into a musical family; some of her most pleasant childhood memories are of singing together, and she says, of singing to the cows – "Oh! How they loved the way I sang…"

**T.S. ELIOT** (Thomas Stearns, 1888-1965) is among the most famous British modernist poets of the 20$^{th}$ century.

**DAVID ELLIS'** poems have appeared widely in literary magazines such as *Laurel Review, Midland Review, Double Entendre, Cimarron Review, America, Crazy Quilt, Licking River Review*, and *Owen Wister Review*. He has won several poetry prizes, including a New York Poetry Forum Award, the Firman Houghton Award from the New England Poetry Club, and the Robert Frost Poetry Festival's International Poem Award. He has published a collection of poems, *Fibonacci's Sequence* and has been a Resident Fellow at the Millay

Colony in New York and at the Virginia Center for the Creative Arts. He teaches English, Creative Writing, and Poetry Workshops at Mount Ida College.
**DONNA L. EMERSON** is a college instructor, licensed clinical social worker, photographer, and writer. Recent or forthcoming poetry publications include *Alembic, California Quarterly, The South Carolina Poetry Review, Chicago Quarterly Review, descant, Fourth River, Illuminations, Schuylkill Valley Journal of the Arts, Paper Street, Foxcry Review, Grasslimb, The Griffin, Phoebe, Sierra Nevada Literary Journal, Marin Poetry Center Anthology, the Paterson Literary Journal, Rio Grande Review, Sixteen Rivers Anthology (2010), So To Speak*, and *Soundings East*. She was a prizewinning flash finalist (2007) for *Tiny Lights* and first prize winner in *California Quarterly's* "Best of the Best," (2008). Her first chapbook, *This Water*, was published in 2007. Finishing Line Press published her second chapbook *Body Rhymes* (June, 2009) for which she has been nominated for a California Book Award. Prose pieces include *L.A. Review, Stone Canoe, Passager*, and *When Last On the Mountain*.

**CHARLES ADÉS FISHMAN** is Emeritus Distinguished Professor of English and Humanities at Farmingdale State College. He has been editor of the Water Mark Poets of North America Book Award, associate editor of *The Drunken Boat*, and poetry editor of *Gaia, Cistercian Studies Quarterly, the Journal of Genocide Research,* and *New Works Review*. Dr. Fishman has also served as poetry consultant to the U.S. Holocaust Memorial Museum, in Washington, DC, since 1995, and is currently poetry editor of *Prism: An Interdisciplinary Journal for Holocaust Educators*. His books include *Water under Water (2009)*; *Blood to Remember: American Poets on the Holocaust* (2007) and *Chopin's Piano* (2006), both from Time Being Books; *Country of Memory* (Uccelli Press, 2004); and *The Death Mazurka* (Texas Tech University Press), a 1989 American Library Association "Outstanding Book of the Year" that was nominated for the 1990 Pulitzer Prize in Poetry. *Chopin's Piano* received the 2007 Paterson Award for Literary Excellence.

**JENNIFER S. FLESCHER'S** poetry publications include *The Harvard Review, Fulcrum, Lit* and the *Blog for the Best American Poetry*. Her non-fiction publications include *Agni-Online, Jubilat, Perihelion,* and *Poetry Daily*. She holds an MFA in poetry, and an MSJ in journalism. She teaches writing and publishing to college students. She is editor and publisher of *Tuesday; An Art Project*. "The Last Words" was nominated for a Pushcart Prize.

**GRETCHEN FLETCHER** won the Poetry Society of America's *Bright Lights, Big Verse* competition and was projected on the Jumbotron as she read her poem in Times Square. She has also been a finalist in the Howard Nemerov Sonnet Competition. Her poetry has been published in numerous journals and anthologies including *upstreet, Chattahoochee Review, Inkwell, The Mid-American Poetry Review*, and *Poetry as Spiritual Practice* by Robert McDowell. She leads writing workshops for Florida Center for the Book, an affiliate of the Library of Congress. Her chapbook, *That Severed Cord* was published by Finishing Line Press.

**LINDA NEMEC FOSTER** is the author of nine collections of poetry including *Amber Necklace from Gdansk* (finalist for the Ohio Book Award in Poetry),

*Listen to the Landscape* (short-listed for the Michigan Notable Book Award), and *Ten Songs from Bulgaria*. Her most recent book, *Talking Diamonds*, was published in 2009 by New Issues Press. Her work has also appeared in numerous journals, magazines, and anthologies including *The Georgia Review*, *Nimrod*, *North American Review*, and *New American Writing*. Foster's poetry has received awards from the Arts Foundation of Michigan, ArtServe Michigan, National Writer's Voice, the Academy of American Poets, and the Polish American Historical Association. She is the founder of the Contemporary Writers Series at Aquinas College and is a member of its program committee.

**EMILY FRAGOS** is an award-winning, widely published poet who teaches poetry writing at New York University and Columbia. She has also taught Shakespeare Studies, poetry, and world literature at Fordham University and the College of Mount Saint Vincent. Fragos is the author of the book of poetry *Little Savage* (Grove/Atlantic, 2004). Her work has appeared in *Best American Poetry*, *The New Yorker*, *Poetry*, *The American Poetry Review*, *Paris Review*, *Threepenny Review*, *Yale Review*, *Boston Review*, *Cimarron Review*, and numerous other journals. She is the editor of three poetry anthologies from Everyman's Pocket Library/Knopf: *The Great Cat*, *The Dance*, and *Music's Spell*. Fragos has also written about dance for *Pointe*, *Bomb*, and *Playbill* magazines. She is the recipient of the David Craig Austin Poetry Prize.

**JAREK GAJEWSKI** is fascinated by inner wanders of the human soul in creation and perception of music and poetry. He plays the trumpet every day and writes poetry occasionally.

**HELEN GRAZIANO** is a poet and founder of Scriblerus Literary Salons in Claremont, California. She published poetry in many issues of the *San Gabriel Valley Poetry Quarterly*, *Phantom Seed*, *Claremont Courier*, and the *Poetry & Cookies* anthologies. In 2009, Palabra Press issued her chapbook, *Woman at Work*. Graziano is often featured at poetry venues in Southern California.

**JOHN Z. GUZLOWSKI's** poetry, fiction, and essays have appeared on *Garrison Kellior's Writers Almanac* and in *The Ontario Review*, *Chattahoochee Review*, *Modern Fiction Studies*, *Nimrod*, *Margie*, *Exquisite Corpse* and other journals here and in Europe. His poems about his Polish parents' experiences in Nazi concentration camps appear in his books *Lightning and Ashes* and *Third Winter of War: Buchenwald*. *Third Winter* was nominated for the Pulitzer Prize in Poetry. He blogs about his parents and their lives at http://lightning-and-ashes.blogspot.com/.

**LOLA HASKINS'** poetry has appeared in *The Atlantic*, the *London Review of Books*, *The New York Quarterly*, *Georgia Review*, *Southern Review*, *Prairie Schooner*, and elsewhere. Her ninth collection of poems, *Still the Mountain* is forthcoming in 2010 from Paper Kite Press. Also forthcoming in 2010, is *Wild Angels*, stories from fifteen Florida cemeteries. In 2007, Ms. Haskins published some poetry advice, *Not Feathers Yet: A Beginner's Guide to the Poetic Life* (Backwaters Press) and a collection of fables about women, with images by Maggie Taylor, *Solutions Beginning with A* (Modernbook). Her most recent books of poems are a new and selected called *Desire Lines* (BOA) and *The*

*Rim Benders* (Anhinga). Ms. Haskins is on the faculty of Rainier Writer's Workshop. For more information, please see www.lolahaskins.com.

**SHAYLA HAWKINS** has published poetry, interviews, book reviews and essays in, among other publications, *Windsor Review, Carolina Quarterly, Yemassee, Poets & Writers Magazine, The Writer, The Ambassador Poetry Project, Paris/Atlantic, Pembroke Magazine* and *Calabash*. Ms. Hawkins has read her poems at the Dodge Poetry Festival and the Library of Congress and is a winner of the Canute A. Brodhurst Prize in Short Fiction from *The Caribbean Writer*. She lives in Detroit, Michigan.

**ELIZABYTH A. HISCOX's** poetry has appeared in numerous journals – most recently *The Fiddlehead* and *Hayden's Ferry Review*. She is the author of the chapbook *Inventory from a One-Hour Room* (2009) from Finishing Line Press. Former poet-in-residence at Durham University U.K., she currently serves as Program Coordinator for the Virginia G. Piper Center for Creative Writing at Arizona State University.

**MARLENE HITT** is a Los Angeles poet, writer, and retired educator, a graduate of Occidental College who also studied at CSUN, UCLA and USC. A 26-year member of Chupa Rosa Writers of Sunland and of California Federation of Chaparral Poets, Ms. Hitt served as Poet-Laureate of Sunland-Tujunga in 1999-2001. Her poetry appeared in *Eclipse, The Vineyard,* and other journals. She published three books on local history, *Sunland-Tujunga From Village to City* (Arcadia Press, 2000 and 2005). She served as a columnist for *The Foothill Leader, Glendale News-Press,* and the *Foothill Paper* (since 1998).

**ROXANNE HOFFMAN** worked on Wall Street, now answers a patient hotline for a major New York home healthcare provider. Her poems and stories appears on and off the net, most recently in *Amaze: The Cinquain Journal, Danse Macabre, The Fib Review, Lucid Rhythms, MOBIUS The Poetry Magazine, Word Slaw* and two anthologies: *The Bandana Republic: A Literary Anthology By Gang Members And Their Affiliates* (Soft Skull Press), and *Love After 70* (Wising Up Press). She and her husband own the small press, POETS WEAR PRADA, www.reverbnation.com/pradapoet

**LAURA L. MAYS HOOPES** lives on the east edge of Los Angeles County in Claremont, CA with her husband, Mike. Her mother attended Julliard and her daughter was a voice major at Boston University, hence her love of music. She was selected for the 2007 A Room of Her Own writing retreat at Ghost Ranch, NM. Hoopes has published nonfiction, short fiction, and poetry in the *North Carolina Literary Review, The Chaffin Journal, Rose City Sisters,* the *Christian Science Monitor, The Scientist, The Writers' Journal, The Writer's Eye, Silhouette* (the forthcoming WriteGirl 2009 anthology), and others. She was awarded a Certificate in Creative Writing from UCLA with Distinction in 2009 and has won several writing contests.

In his somewhat wasted youth, **G. BENNETT HUMPHREY** received a MD and PhD from the University of Chicago, a disfiguring experience that turned his head into an egg. In his not so wasted youth, Ben studied piano, trumpet and later the banjo. Music was and still is an escape into solitude. Ben is pleased to have an opportunity to participate in this tribute to Chopin. He has been a guest on several occasions in Poland and wishes to express his gratitude for the hospitality that was extended to him by the Polish people. A retired Professor of Pediatric Oncology, Ben has been writing poetry since 2005. His poems have been published in American and British Journals and anthologies. He is an active member of Poetry West and serves on its Board of Directors.

**ORIANA IVY** was born in Poland and came to the United States when she was 17. Her poems, essays, book reviews, and translations from modern Polish poetry have been published in *Poetry, Ploughshares, Best American Poetry 1992, Nimrod, New Letters, The Iowa Review, American Poetry Review, Black Warrior, Wisconsin Review, Prairie Schooner, Spoon River Review, Southern Poetry Review,* and many other journals and anthologies. A former journalist and community college instructor, she now teaches creative writing workshops. She lives in San Diego.

**CAROL J. JENNINGS** is an attorney at the Federal Trade Commission in Washington DC, working in consumer protection. She received both her undergraduate and law degrees from New York University. She has published poems in various journals, including *The New York Quarterly, The Potomac Review, Oberon,* and the *Chautauqua Literary Journal.* Ms. Jennings was on the editorial staff of *The New York Quarterly* in the early years of its publication. She also plays the piano.

**CHARLOTTE JONES** worked for many years as a management consultant before deciding to do something more creative with her life and started writing. Her poetry has appeared in numerous literary magazines including *The Bellevue Literary Review, Nerve Cowboy, Barbaric Yawp, The Texas Poetry Calendar,* and *The Bayou Review.* She also writes short stories, essays, nonfiction and short plays. She is currently at work on her first novel.

**LOIS P. JONES** has been published in *Rose & Thorn, The California Quarterly, Kyoto Journal, Prism Review, Arsenic Lobster* and other print and on-line journals in the U.S. and abroad. She is the co-founder of Word Walker Press with Alice Pero and a recent documentarist of Argentina's wine industry. In 2008, she was the recipient of IBPC's first prize honor judged by Fleda Brown. You can find her as co-producer at *Moonday's* monthly poetry reading in Pacific Palisades, California and hear her as host on 90.7 KPFK's Poet's Cafe in Los Angeles, California. She is the Associate Poetry Editor of *Kyoto Journal* and a 2009 Pushcart nominee.

**GEORGIA JONES-DAVIS** wakes up in the morning thinking about poetry as much as breakfast. That she began, whilst a student, to compose poetry at the same time that she started to listen to the music of Chopin is no coincidence, she insists. She spent over twenty years rough-housing it in journalism, working as a reporter, book review editor and literary reviewer for *The Los Angeles Times, The Washington Post, New York Newsday* and *The Chicago Tribune,* among other publications. Georgia is squarely focused on poetry now and still listening to Chopin. Her work has appeared in *West Wind,*

*The Bicycle Review, Brevities, Voices From the Valley, The Los Angeles Times* and the *California Quarterly*. She is a co-director of Valley Contemporary Poets (VCP) and at work on her first book of poems.

**CHRISTINE KLOCEK-LIM** received the 2009 Ellen La Forge Memorial Prize in poetry. In 2006 her work was a finalist in *Nimrod's* Pablo Neruda Prize for Poetry, in 2009 her work was a semi-finalist in the Brittingham and Pollak Poetry Prizes (University of Wisconsin Press), a semi-finalist at the Philip Levine Prize in Poetry, and a semi-finalist at the Black Lawrence Press' Black River Chapbook Competition. She has two chapbooks: *How to photograph the heart (*The Lives You Touch Publications) and *The book of small treasures* (Seven Kitchens Press). Her poems have appeared in *Nimrod, Poets and Artists (O&S), Riffing on Strings: Creative Writing Inspired by String Theory* and elsewhere. She edits *Autumn Sky Poetry.* Website: www.novembersky.com.

**JEAN L. KREILING's** poetry has appeared in several print and on-line journals, including *Contemporary Sonnet, Dogwood, Ekphrasis, The Evansville Review, The Formalist, The Pennsylvania Review,* and *SLANT*. In her other life, she teaches music at Bridgewater State College in Massachusetts; she previously taught English at Western Carolina University in North Carolina. Her academic work includes presentations on music and poetry at recent conferences in Baltimore, Boston, Honolulu, Toronto, and London.

**LEONARD KRESS** published five poetry collections; the latest is *The Orpheus Complex* (Main Street Rag Press). He translated Mickiewicz's complete *Pan Tadeusz*, which is available as a free pdf download from HarrowGatePress: www.harrowgatepress.com. Kress currently teaches philosophy, religion, and creative writing at Owens College in Ohio.

**EMMA LAZARUS** (1849-1887) is an American poet, born in New York City and best known for *The New Colossus*, a sonnet written in 1883 and partly engraved on the Statue of Liberty. Lazarus came from a prominent Jewish family, knew many languages, edited works of Goethe and Heine for American publications. She wrote a novel, two plays, and translations of Jewish poetry.

**MARIE LECRIVAIN** is the executive editor and publisher of *poeticdiversity: the litzine of Los Angeles* and is a writer in residence at her apartment. Her prose and poetry have appeared in a number of journals and anthologies, including: *Aesthetica, I Left This Here for You, Luces y Sombras, Media Cake eMagazine, NEONBEAM, Poetic Voices Without Borders 2* (copyright 2009 Gival Press), *The Poetry Salzburg Review, Re)verb, The Los Angeles Review, Sein Und Werden, The Toronto Quarterly*, and is forthcoming in *Spillway,* and *Dashboard Horus: A Bird's Eye of the Universe.* Her short story, "The Word Thief" was nominated for a 2007 Pushcart Prize. Marie's new poetry collection, *Antibellum Messiah* (Sybaritic Press, 2009), is available through Amazon.com.

**JEFFREY LEVINE** is the author of two books of poetry, *Rumor of Cortez* (Red Hen Press, 2005) nominated for an LA Times Book Award in Poetry, and *Mortal, Everlasting*, winner of the Transcontinental Poetry Prize (Pavement Saw Press, 2002). A third is book due out in 2010. Thirteen times nominated for a Pushcart Prize, he has won the Larry Levis Prize from *The Missouri Review, North American Review's* James Hearst Poetry Prize, the *Mississippi Review Poetry Prize,* the *Kestrel Poetry Prize,* the *Ekphrasis* Prize, and most recently, the 2008 *National Poetry Journal* Award, among others. A graduate of the Warren Wilson MFA Program for Writers, he is Editor-in-Chief and Publisher of Tupelo Press, an independent literary press with offices in North Adams, Massachusetts, now celebrating its 10th anniversary year.

**AMY LOWELL** (1874-1925) was an American poet belonging to imagistic school, who published over 650 poems and won the Pulitzer Prize for Poetry after her premature death. Her books include: *A Dome of Many-Colored Glass* (1912), *Sword Blades and Poppy Seed* (1914), *Men, Women and Ghosts* (1916), and *Pictures from a Floating World* (1919). She also wrote literary criticism, translations from ancient Chinese poetry, and a biography of Keats.

**R. ROMEA LUMINARIAS** (Rey Luminarias) studied architecture and poetry in Manila, Hong Kong, China, Seattle and Los Angeles, California. His works have appeared in various publications, including issues of the *Caracoa Literay Journal* and the *San Gabriel Valley Poetry Quarterly.* His poems have been included in an anthology, *Philippine Protest Poetry.* A member of Poets West, Rey Luminarias is also a painter and paper sculptor. He teaches architecture, painting, marimba music, creative writing, and finds fulfillment in sharing his life and working with disadvantaged children, the developmentally disabled and the infirm elderly. Rey's collection of large-print meditative writings and an illustrated book of poems and riddles are forthcoming this year.

**RICK LUPERT** has been involved with poetry in Los Angeles since 1990. He served for two years as a co-director of the Valley Contemporary Poets, a 30-year San Fernando Valley based literary organization. His poetry has appeared in places such as *The Los Angeles Times, Chiron Review, Stirring, The Blue Jew Yorker, PoeticDiversity.org, Caffeine Magazine, Blue Satellite* and others. He edited *A Poet's Haggadah: Passover through the Eyes of Poets* anthology and is the author of 12 poetry collections. He has hosted the weekly Cobalt Café reading series in Canoga Park since 1994 and is regularly featured at venues throughout Southern California. Rick created and maintains the Poetry Super Highway, an online resource and publication for poets. (PoetrySuperHighway.com) Currently Rick works as the music teacher and graphic/web designer for a synagogue in Northridge, CA and for anyone who would like to help pay his mortgage. He lives in Van Nuys, CA with his wife Addie, son Jude, three cats, a lizard and a frog.

**RADOMIR VOJTECH LUZA** is a friend to peasants and poets, senators and saints. His poetry is breaking ground at warp speed and possessing enough images and details to stand in museums for hundreds of years and millions of minutes. Radomir has published poetry in literary journals, anthologies and websites; he hosted *po-rap* (his own music form) readings all over the country. He has fifteen poetry and prose books to his credit, of which the last one is *Damaged Goods.* His poetry recently appeared in *Phantom Seed, Sage Trail, The Bicycle Review* and *poeticdiversity.* His featured poetry gigs took place in

New York City, Philadelphia, New Orleans, Washington DC, Atlanta, Los Angeles, St. Louis, Northwest Florida, Pensacola, FL and Biloxi, MS.

**MIRA (MIRJANA) N. MATARIC** is a Californian poet and writer from Serbia. She earned her M.A. and Ph.D. in languages and world literature at the University of Belgrade and, after immigrating to the U.S. in 1981, pursued a Master's in Special Education from Emporia University, KS. Her poetry, short stories, translations (Serbian/ English), essays and travelogues have appeared in literary magazines and journals for decades. Mira has published 30 books in English and Serbian, including her own poetry and prose, as well as many translations. Her writings offer a vibrant, picturesque, true depiction of life and people in times of strife and joy, always filled with wisdom, beauty and love of life. She received numerous awards for poetry in the United States and Serbia, as well as three Presidential Citations for her volunteer work in advancing literature and teaching creative writing. www.mitamataric.net

The author of three books of poetry, **RYAN MCLELLAN** is a performance poet, singer/songwriter and English teacher from New Hampshire. His work has been published in the *2010 Poets' Guide to New Hampshire, OVS Magazine, Bird's Eye reView, Essence* and *Concise Delight.* The recipient of the 2009 Esther Buffler Memorial Fellowship and member of the 2009 *Slam Free or Die* team, he has spent the last year touring and presenting workshops on slam and spoken word to high school students around New England.

Polish-born **ANNA MARIA MICKIEWICZ** lives and writes in Great Britain (London). Her first collection of poetry, *Dziewanna,* was published in 1984 in Poland. She is a member of The Union of Polish Writers Abroad and edits its annual literary magazine, *Pamiętnik Literacki*. In the year 2000 she published a book in Poland, *The Crumbs from the Round Table.* Her prose and poetry appear in a literary journal "Akant". She also contributes literary essays to academic volumes.

**ELISABETH MURAWSKI** is the author of *Moon and Mercury* and a chapbook, *Troubled by an Angel.* Her poetry has appeared in *The Yale Review, The New Republic, Virginia Quarterly Review, The Ontario Review, The Literary Review, Field, Chelsea, Margie,* and others. Her poem "Abu Ghraib Suggests the Isenheim Altarpiece" won the 2006 Ann Stanford Prize. She was awarded a Hawthornden fellowship in 2008. Born and raised in Chicago, she attended De Paul University and received an MFA from George Mason University. She resides in Alexandria, VA. While in Paris in 1998 she tracked down places where Chopin lived and also visited his grave at Père Lachaise and the Polish Museum where his armchair is preserved along with first editions, the death mask, and a lock of his hair. Naturally, he is her favorite composer!

**RUTH NOLAN**, M.A., is founder of *Phantom Seed*, a California desert literary magazine. She was born in San Bernardino, grew up in the high desert town of Apple Valley, and worked as a helicopter hotshot firefighter for the Bureau of Land Management during her college years. She currently lives in Palm Desert, where she is Associate Professor of English at College of the Desert. She is editor of a new anthology, *No Place for a Puritan: the literature of California's*

*Deserts,* forthcoming from Heyday Books in fall, 2009. She is recipient of a 2008-09 Joshua Tree National Park affiliate writer's residency, and has published several collections of poetry, including *Wild Wash Road,* and *Dry Waterfall I.* Her poetry has appeared in numerous literary magazines, including, recently, *Pacific Review.* She serves on the advisory committee for the Inlandia Institute, based in Riverside, CA.

**CYPRIAN KAMIL NORWID** (1821-1883), is a Polish romantic poet, playwright and sculptor, considered the fourth "wieszcz" – prophetic poet-bard, along with Adam Mickiewicz, Juliusz Słowacki and Zygmunt Krasiński. An author of symbolic, mystical, often hermetic poetry featuring complex literary devices and rich symbolism, Norwid spent most of his life as an emigrant in London and Paris. His poetry was misunderstood by his contemporaries and first appreciated by the Young Poland generation in the 20$^{th}$ century. His poem, *Fortepian Szopena* has never been translated into English.

**ROSEMARY O'HARA** is a Seattle poet. She has had careers in nursing and as a marriage and family therapist. She is currently studying piano at Cornish College of the Arts. Her work has appeared in local and national journals, including *Willow Review, Spindrift, Between the Lines,* and *Vox Populi,* 2007. A chapbook, *Knots of Clouds,* was published by Finishing line Press, 2007.

**DEAN PASCH** was born on March 4 in 1963—it was a Monday. No one could tell him what time it was and this vagueness has threaded its way through his life. Where do facts begin and end? How much information does one need to be able to make an incontestable statement of fact? He was born—of that he can be certain. At some point the notion of a career (in anything) became worrying, and he un-hitched himself from that trajectory and set sail on a voyage he is still on. If he were to label himself as anything other than a human being, it would be as an artist pursuing art in whatever ways are possible whilst staying true to his senses and imagination. He writes poetry, stories, draws and makes films. He lives in Munich, Germany. His work has appeared in *Mannequin Envy* and *Niederngasse.*

**NILS PETERSON** is Professor Emeritus at San Jose State University where he taught in the English and Humanities Departments. He has published poetry, science fiction, and articles on subjects as varying as golf and Shakespeare. A chapbook of poems entitled *Here Is No Ordinary Rejoicing* was published by No Deadlines Press, a collection of poems entitled *The Comedy of Desire* with an introduction by Robert Bly was published by the Blue Sofa Press, a collection of poems entitled *Driving a Herd of Moose to Durango* appeared in 2005, and *For This Day* in 2008. In 2009, he was chosen to be the first Poet Laureate of Santa Clara County.

**RICHARD PFLUM** has published five books of poetry: *Moving Into the Light* (1975), *A Dream of Salt* (1980), *A Strange Juxtaposition of Parts* (1995) and *Listening with Others* (2007), and *The Haunted Refrigerator and Other Poems,* 2007. Pflum's poems appear in regional and national anthologies: *Glassworks, A New Geography of Poets, The Indiana Experience,* and *Bear Crossings.* He taught as part time instructor of Advanced Poetry Writing at IUPUI during the late 1980's. He currently runs a Poetry Salon for The Writers' Center of Indiana in Indianapolis. Pflum wanted to be a musician and composer but found his talent more suited to words.

Born in the Ukraine and displaced by Russian pogroms and World War I, **WILLIAM PILLIN** (1910-1985) was a poet and potter. published nine books of poetry including: *Theory of Silence* (1949), *Passage at Midnight* (Inferno Press Editions, 1958), *Pavane for a Fading Memory* (Alan Swallow, 1973), *The Abandoned Music Room* (Kayak Press, 1975), *To the End of Time* (Papa Bach Editions, 1980), and *Another Dawn* (Iluminati, 1984). His books were frequently illustrated by artwork by his wife, Polia Pillin (1909-1992), a Polish-American artist known for her ceramics with original glazes and decorations. Pillin also collaborated with his wife in creating art pottery.

**KENNETH POBO** won the 2009 Main Street Rag poetry chapbook contest for his manuscript called *Trina and the Sky*. It was published in December 2009. In 2008, WordTech Press published his book called *Glass Garden*. He teaches Creative Writing and English at Widener University in Pennsylvania.

**CARRIE A. PURCELL** holds an MFA in Poetry from the University of Washington. Her poems have appeared in *Crate, Faultline The Dudley Review*, and *Inknode*. She is a member of the arts non-profit, The Heroes, and lives in Seattle.

**MARILYN N. ROBERTSON** lives in Northeast Los Angeles. She has studied with Suzanne Lummis and been a featured reader at the "Viva Poetry" series leading up to Lummis Day in NELA, at the Light the Sky poetry series at the Eagle Rock Plaza, and at the Pat Pincus Memorial Poetry Readings in Brentwood. Her poetry appears in the forthcoming book, *The Poetry Mystique* published by Duende Books. She is a graduate of Occidental College in English Literature, with Masters' and doctoral degrees in education from USC. She was a president of the California School Library Association. During her 34 years with the Los Angeles Unified School District, she served students as one of the district librarians specializing in storytelling and children's literature.

**SUSAN ROGERS** considers poetry a vehicle for light and a tool for the exchange of positive energy. She is a practitioner of Sukyo Mahikari—a spiritual practice that promotes positive thoughts, words and action. www.sukyomahikari.org. Her poems will be part of the 2010 Valentine Peace Project and were part of the 2009 event "Celebrating Women: Body, Mind and Spirit." They have also been performed at several museums and art galleries in Southern California. Her work can be found in the 2009 haiku anthology, *Shell Gathering*, numerous chapbooks from Poets on Site and can be heard online as part of the audio tour for the Pacific Asia Museum in Pasadena, California.

**ALISON ROSS** venerates verse. She has published poetry in various print journals and webzines. Alison also praises political polemics, and has written radical "rants" and scathing satire for such sites as *Exquisite Corpse* and *Democracy Means You*. Alison is the editor of the online progressive literary magazine, *Clockwise Cat*.

**MARY RUDGE** is the Poet Laureate of the City of Alameda, California USA and International Poet Laureate (member of United Poets Laureate International). She speaks internationally on Creating Peace and Poetry as a Healing Art. Her poetry has been performed in dance on stages round the world. She received honorary doctorates in Canada, New York and the Republic of China, was named Princess of Poetry in Italy, crowned with gold laureate from a Poet Laureate of Peru and with a laureate crown at San Francisco City Hall by United Poets Laureate International. She became the first Poet Laureate of the city of Alameda in 2002. Some of her work has been widely translated and published. Her books include: *Water Planet; Hungary, Austria and Other Passions*; and *The Skin of God*.

**RUSSELL SALAMON** has been writing poetry since 1963 when at Fenn College in Cleveland, Ohio he discovered his purpose to create art in words. He has written a poetic novel about the Sixties, *Descent into Cleveland*, (Words and Pictures Press, 1994). Two books of poems *Woodsmoke* and *Green Tea* (deepclevelandpress 2006) and *Ascent from Cleveland: Wild Heart Steel Phoenix,* (Bottom Dog Press with Fredonia Press 2008) are still in print. *Breeze Hunting*, a chapbook (Inevitable Press 2001) exists. Author of many poems, most recently the *Black Axioms Series* of love poems. He is one of the editors of *California Quarterly*, having just selected for Volume 36, Number 1.

**GABRIEL SHANKS** is a writer, poet, photographer and stage director based in New York City. The recipient of the Theatre Project Honor for Outstanding Vision and the Maxim Mazumdar New Play Award, Gabriel was one of the directors of *The Village Fragments*, which was honored with a 2007 Obie Award. His first poetry collection, *GlitterDirt*, will be published in 2010 (http://www.gabrielshanks.com/glitterdirt). He lives with his partner of seventeen years, Dennis.

Born in 1939 in a housing project in The Bronx, **MARIAN KAPLUN SHAPIRO** practices as a psychologist and poet in Lexington, Massachusetts. The author of *Second Childhood* (Norton, 1988) and many professional articles, in the last few years her poems have appeared in over 150 journals and anthologies, and have won twenty first prizes and many other prizes. Her book, *Players In The Dream, Dreamers In The Play* appeared in April, 2007 from Plain View Press, and her chapbook, *Parenthesis,* appears on the website of Language And Culture (www.languageandculture.net) Her chapbooks, *Your Third Wish,* (Finishing Line), and *The End Of The World, Announced On Wednesday* (Pudding House) also appeared in late 2007. She was named Senior Poet Laureate of Massachusetts in 2006 and again in 2008.

**LUSIA SLOMKOWSKA** is a poet, essayist, and translator. She has traveled, lived, and taught in Eastern Europe as well as a variety of locations in the United States. She has taught and directed programs at Phoenix College, the Experiment in International Living, Brattleboro, Vermont; Freehand in Provincetown, Massachusetts, and improvisational theater at the Yale Cabaret Theatre in New Haven, Connecticut. Her poetry has been published in a variety of journals, including *The Agni Review* and *Parnassus*. Her work has been anthologized, and has won various awards and fellowships. Her current translation project includes several contemporary Polish poets with a critical introduction. She has also worked as an actuary, bread packer, dental assistant, and produce farmer.

Originally from Spain, **JOSEPH SOMOZA** retired from teaching college English years ago and lives in Las Cruces, New Mexico, with wife Jill, a painter. He published several books and chapbooks of poetry, most recently *Shock of White Hair* (Sin Fronteras Press, 2007). The "Chopin Etude" previously appeared in *Out of This World* (Cinco Puntos Press, El Paso, 1990).

**KATHI STAFFORD's** poetry has appeared in various literary journals such as *Chiron Review, Nerve Cowboy, Offerings,* and *Hard Row to Hoe.* She is poetry editor for Southern California Review. Additionally, she is a Pushcart Prize nominee for 2009. She is a graduate of the Master of Professional Writing program at the University of Southern California.

**MAXINE R. SYJUCO** is a poet, transmedia artist and fashion model based in the Philippines. At 24, she is considered to be one of the most prolific and prominent poets / performance artists to emerge from the Philippine art and literary scenes in recent years. Her first book of poetry, A Secret Life, was published in 2008. In 2009, she had her first solo visual arts exhibition entitled "A Post-Traumatic Stress Disorder." Maxine Syjuco is currently the frontwoman of the experimental art-band 'Utakan', performing her poetry and music in numerous venues around the Philippines, including art museums, galleries, concert halls, etc.

**FIONA SZE-LORRAIN** is the author of *Water the Moon* (Marick Press, 2010). She is an editor at *Cerise Press*, a guzheng concert artist and a classical pianist. She writes and translates in English, French and Chinese. Her poems appear in *Caesura, Ellipsis, Santa Clara Review, New Politics, Raven Chronicles, Tibetan Review,* and other journals. She lives in Paris, France (www.fionasze.com).

**MARGARET C. SZUMOWSKI** grew up in Winterset, Iowa, graduated from the University of Iowa and shortly thereafter took off for the Peace Corps and served in the Congo and Ethiopia. As a hostage in Uganda, she had the distinction of having her photo taken by Idi Amin—a sort of keepsake for him. Szumowski received her MFA from the University of Massachusetts, and was a full professor at an inner city community college, Springfield Technical Community College, teaching English and writing. She published three books of poetry: *Ruby's Café* (Devil's Millhopper Press, 1991), *I Want this World* (Tupelo Press, 2001) and *Night of the Lunar Eclipse* (Tupelo Press, 2005).

Australian-born **KATRIN TALBOT's** collection *St. Cecilia's Daze* is forthcoming from Parallel Press. She was recently nominated for a Pushcart Prize in Poetry 2009. Her poetry has appeared in *The New Plains Review, Inertia, Ginosko, Fresh Ink, Free Verse, Your Daily Poem,* Ragged Sky Press's *Eating her Wedding Dress, Empty Shoes, And Again Last Night,* and *Not A Muse* Anthologies, and will appear in the *Zoland, If,* and *Manorborn Poetry Journals,* and in the upcoming anthologies *Collecting Life, Vicious Verses and*

*Reanimated Rhyme, The Bridges of New York, Tribute to Orpheus II* and *The Poetry of Travel*. She was a finalist in 2009 for four national poetry prizes.

Long-time educator, published author and artist, **TAOLI-AMBIKA TALWAR** has been involved in holistic arts/sciences for many years. She practices Yuen Method, DNA/Thetahealing™ and polarity therapy. Language, she believes, is key to our healing and renewal. "Both poetry and holistic work beautifully together. I see the power of language coded in us and help you to find and be in your resonance, for then we choose rightly", noting that language matters— language of the mind, body, spirit and beyond. She has published poems in various journals, gained some renown in the Los Angeles area as a poet, and made a film for which she won the best script award at a festival in Belgium. Taoli-Ambika currently resides in Los Angeles and enjoys travelling to India, to eternal inner landscapes, and to a little place of laughter—happy medicine. "Keep that smile glowing!" http://www.goldenmatrixvisions.com

**THOM TAMMARO** teaches at Minnesota State University Moorhead, where he is Professor of English, a co-founder of the MFA in Creative Writing, and a Roland and Beth Dille Distinguished Faculty Lecturer. He is the author of four collections of poems and co-editor of six anthologies of poetry, most recently *To Sing Along the Way: Minnesota Women Poets from Pre-Territorial Days to the Present*. His poems, essays, reviews and interviews have appeared in such journals as *American Poetry Review, The Chronicle of Higher Education, College Composition and Communication,* and *The Emily Dickinson Journal*.

**MARK TARDI** is the author of *Euclid Shudders*, a finalist for the 2002 National Poetry Series that was published by Litmus Press. He also wrote two chapbooks *Airport music* (Bronze Skull, 2005) and *Part First-----Chopin's Feet* (g-o-n-g, 2005). Recent work of his can be found in *Chicago Review, Van Gogh's Ear,* and the anthology *The City Visible: Chicago Poetry for the New Millennium*. He is on the editorial board of *Aufgabe,* an international literary journal, where he is coordinating a project devoted to the work and influence of Polish poet Miron Białoszewski on contemporary poetry. He was the 2008/2009 Senior Fulbright Lecturer in American Literature & Culture at the University of Łódź, and his *Airport Music* is forthcoming from Burning Deck Press.

**CHERYL M. THATT** is an English teacher and a graduate of San Francisco State University's Creative Writing program. In 2008, she was selected to participate in College of the Canyons annual "Poets and Writers" series. She loves and is inspired by Jean Yves Thibaudet's CD, "The Chopin I Love." She lives with her husband and two children in Valencia, California.

**TAMMY L. TILLOTSON's** poetry has appeared in *Sweetbay Review* 2008 and won an honorable mention in the Writer's Eye 2008 and the 2009 Wergle Flomp Humor Poetry Contest. She is the editor of the Writers Studio Young Authors Anthology, entitled *Bull Bay Review*. She earned her Bachelor of Science degree from Old Dominion University and her Master of Arts in Liberal Studies from Hollins University.

**MAJA TROCHIMCZYK** is a poet, music historian, photographer and translator born in Poland, educated in Warsaw and at McGill University in Canada (Ph.D., 1994), and living in California (www.trochimczyk.net). She received fellowships and awards from SSHRC, ACLS, and PAHA. She published four books of music studies (*After Chopin*; *The Music of Louis Andriessen*; *Polish Dance in Southern California*, and *A Romantic Century in Polish Music*), two books of poetry illustrated with her photographs (*Rose Always* and *Miriam's Iris*, 2008), hundreds of peer-reviewed and popular articles on music and culture, and over 70 poems in *Magnapoets, poeticdiversity, San Gabriel Valley Poetry Quarterly, Quill & Parchment, Ekprasis,* and anthologies by Poets on Site and others. She taught music history at McGill University and USC, served as editor-in-chief for *Polish Music Journal,* and founded Moonrise Press.

**HELEN VANDEPEER** is a published playwright, poet and author. Her play, "After the Fair" was a winner in the UNESCO playwright competition in 2002. The play was published and performed in play readings in Greece, Turkey and the U.S. Other published works include children's books, poems and short stories. Ms. Vandepeer is an Australian now living in North Ontario, Canada, married to the love of her life whom she met on the writing site Blogit.

**DAVI WALDERS'** poetry and prose have appeared in more than 200 anthologies and journals, including *The American Scholar, JAMA, Ms Magazine, Crab Orchard Review, Seneca Review, Lonely Planet, Travelers' Tales,* and elsewhere. She developed and directs the Vital Signs Writing Project at NIH in Bethesda, MD which was funded for three years by The Witter Bynner Foundation for Poetry. She received Greater Washington Hadassah's Myrtle Wreath Award for the Project which was featured in *JAMA* and other publications. Her awards include a National Endowment for the Humanities Grant, a Puffin Foundation Grant, a Maryland State Artist Grant in Poetry, a Luce Foundation Grant, and fellowships to Ragdale Foundation, Blue Mountain Center, Virginia Center for the Creative Arts. Her work has been choreographed and performed in NYC and elsewhere, read by Garrison Keillor on *Writer's Almanac,* and nominated for Pushcart Prizes.

**ERIKA WILK** is a poet, born in Bavaria, raised in Salzburg, Austria, and for the past fifty years a California girl. She is a member of two poetry groups based in Pasadena, Emerging Urban Poets and Poets on Site. Her poetry has been published in the *San Gabriel Valley Poetry Quarterly* and several chapbooks by Poets on Site, written to paintings by Milford Zornes, Henry Fukuhara, etc.

**MARTIN WILLITTS, JR.** was nominated for four Pushcart Awards. His recent poems appeared in *Blue Fifth, Parting Gifts, Bent Pin, New Verse* news, *Storm at Galesburg and other stories* (anthology), *The Centrifugal Eye, Quiddity, Autumn Sky Poetry, Protest Poems,* and others. His tenth chapbook was *The Garden of French Horns* (Pudding House Publications, 2008) and his second full length book of poetry is *The Hummingbird* (March Street Press, 2009). He has two forthcoming chapbooks: *Baskets of Tomorrow"*(Flutter Press, 2009) and *True Simplicity* (Poets Wear Prada Press, 2010).

**KATH ABELA WILSON** is the creator and leader of Poets on Site, a poetry performance group where poets collaborate with dancers, musicians, and artists to perform on site of their inspirations, including museums and galleries. She edited 14 chapbooks of Poets of Site including hundreds of poems. Her poetry appeared in *The California Quarterly, Prism, Tinywords, Asahi, Astro Poetica, Haiku News, Ribbons, Red Lights, Shakespeare's Monkey Revue, Pirate Pig Press, Star\*Line, astarte, lunarosity, Totem, Phantom Seed*, and in various anthologies. She sings in the alto section in the Caltech Glee Club and fell in love with Chopin as a young girl. Without a piano, she learned to play some of his pieces on a paper keyboard, for her weekly lessons. She often travels the world with her Caltech math professor husband Rick Wilson and they both collect musical instruments, antique and world flutes and percussion.

**LEONORE WILSON** teaches English literature at a private university in San Francisco. Her work has been in such magazines as *Quarterly West, Madison Review, Third Coast, Pif, Magma*, etc.

**MEG WITHERS** is a writer, teacher, and community activist. She writes when she can – usually in between correcting homework and encouraging the community where she lives to take action on civil rights issues. She currently conducts labors of love+discipline at Merced Community College District. She pets her lovely cat, Fred-O, all the time. She has books of poetry: *Must Be Present to Win* (Ghost Road Press, 2006), and *A Communion of Saints* (TinFish Press, 2008). She has been published in major journals, and has been nationally anthologized. She earned both her MA (2005), and MFA (2008), from San Francisco State University. She is currently editing an anthology, *Shadowed: The Disappearing Woman,* in partnership with Joell Hallowell, utilizing black and white photos, honoring women with prose poems by women poets. Her other current projects include the adaptation of *The Communion of Saints* as a play, and etymological feminist poems utilizing Chaucer's Middle English, to be entitled, *The Etymology of Desire.*

**ANNE HARDING WOODWORTH** is the author of three books of poetry and two chapbooks. Her most recent book is *SPARE PARTS, A Novella in Verse* (Turning Point, 2008). Her essays and poetry have appeared in U.S. and Canadian journals, such as *TriQuarterly, Painted Bride Quarterly, Connecticut Review, Antigonish Review,* and *Poet Lore,* as well as at several sites online. She holds an MFA in poetry from Fairleigh Dickinson University and is a member of the Poetry Board at the Folger Shakespeare Library. www.annehardingwoodworth.com

**MARIANNE WORTHINGTON** is the author of the poetry collection *Larger Bodies Than Mine* (Finishing Line Press, 2006) and editor of *MOTIF: Writing by Ear, An Anthology of Writings about Music* (Motes Books, 2009). She teaches writing, communication and journalism in Williamsburg, Kentucky.

# INDEX OF POETS

Millicent Borges **Accardi,** 11, 26, 204
Austin **Alexis,** 126, 204
Lucy **Anderton,** 95, 204
Sheila **Black,** 161, 204
George **Bodmer,** 138, 204
Lia **Brooks,** 98, 204
Kerri **Buckley,** 23, 97, 200, 204
Allison **Campbell,** 182, 205
Peggy **Castro,** 177, 205
Sharon **Chmielarz,** 81, 171, 191, 205
Victor **Contoski,** 105, 205
Clark **Crouch,** 80, 205
Beata **Poźniak Daniels,** 124, 206
Jessica **Day,** 28, 206
Diane Shipley **DeCillis,** 169, 206
Lori **Desrosiers,** 70, 206
Charlie **Durrant,** 180, 206
T. S. **Eliot,** 164, 206
David **Ellis,** 90, 206
Donna L. **Emerson,** 152, 162, 207
Charles Adés **Fishman,** 22, 207
Jennifer S. **Flescher,** 92, 139, 207
Gretchen **Fletcher,** 112, 207
Linda Nemec **Foster,** 88, 207
Emily **Fragos,** 84, 202, 208
Jarek **Gajewski,** 91, 208
Helen **Graziano,** 127, 208
John Z. **Guzlowski,** 64, 208
Lola **Haskins,** 104, 208
Shayla **Hawkins,** 109, 209
Elizabyth A. **Hiscox,** 201, 209
Marlene **Hitt,** 75, 184, 209
Roxanne **Hoffman,** 27, 209
Laura L. Mays **Hoopes,** 135, 209
Ben **Humphrey,** 36, 74, 210
Oriana **Ivy,** 198, 210
Carol J. **Jennings,** 136, 210
Charlotte **Jones,** 154, 210
Lois P. **Jones,** 71, 156, 210
Georgia **Jones-Davis,** 133, 210
Christine **Klocek-Lim,** 32, 211
Jean L. **Kreiling,** 108, 211
Leonard **Kress,** 16, 30, 211
Emma **Lazarus,** 4, 211
Marie **Lecrivain,** 101-103, 211

Jeffrey **Levine,** 119, 212
Amy **Lowell,** 6, 212
R. Romea **Luminarias,** 44, 212
Rick **Lupert,** 176, 212
Radomir V. **Luza,** 144, 197, 212
Mira N. **Mataric,** 149, 190, 213
Ryan **McLellan,** 174, 178, 213
Anna Maria **Mickiewicz,** 175, 213
Elisabeth **Murawski,** 42, 62, 86, 213
Ruth **Nolan,** 116, 214
Cyprian Kamil **Norwid,** 16, 214
Rosemary **O'Hara,** 93, 214
Dean **Pasch,** 73, 214
Nils **Peterson,** 40, 214
Richard **Pflum,** 34, 115, 215
William **Pillin,** 8, 215
Kenneth **Pobo,** 140, 215
Carrie A. **Purcell,** 38, 215
Marilyn N. **Robertson,** 148, 215
Susan **Rogers,** 155, 215
Alison **Ross,** 13, 216
Mary **Rudge,** 186, 216
Russell **Salamon,** 72, 106, 216
Gabriel **Shanks,** 66, 216
Marian Kaplun **Shapiro,** 193, 216
Joseph **Somoza,** 43, 217
Lusia **Slomkowska,** 129, 217
Kathi **Stafford,** 54, 123, 217
Maxine R. **Syjuco,** 14, 217
Fiona **Sze-Lorrain,** 142, 217
Margaret C. **Szumowski,** 168, 217
Katrin **Talbot,** 56, 58, 192, 218
Taoli-Ambika **Talwar,** 77, 82, 218
Thom **Tammaro,** 172, 218
Mark **Tardi,** 47, 218
Cheryl M. **Thatt,** 35, 218
Tammy L. **Tillotson,** 120-122, 219
Maja **Trochimczyk,** 45, 57, 59, 219
Helen **Vandepeer,** 179, 219
Devi **Walders,** 189, 219
Erika **Wilk,** 130, 145, 219
Martin **Willitts, Jr.,** 24, 131, 159, 219
Kath Abela **Wilson,** 67, 220
Leonore **Wilson,** 100, 118, 195, 220
Meg **Withers,** 111, 220
Anne Harding **Woodworth,** 143, 220
Marianne **Worthington,** 39, 220

www.ingramcontent.com/pod-product-compliance
Lightning Source LLC
Chambersburg PA
CBHW022004160426
43197CB00007B/270